Middle School General Music

The Best Part of Your Day

ELIZABETH ANN MCANALLY

Published in partnership with
MENC: The National Association for Music Education

ROWMAN & LITTLEFIELD EDUCATION
A division of
ROWMAN & LITTLEFIELD PUBLISHERS, INC.
Lanham • New York • Toronto • Plymouth, UK

Published in partnership with MENC: The National Association for Music Education

Published by Rowman & Littlefield Education
A division of Rowman & Littlefield Publishers, Inc.
A wholly owned subsidiary of The Rowman & Littlefield Publishing Group, Inc.
4501 Forbes Boulevard, Suite 200, Lanham, Maryland 20706
http://www.rowmaneducation.com

Estover Road, Plymouth PL6 7PY, United Kingdom

British Library Cataloguing in Publication Information Available

Library of Congress Cataloging-in-Publication Data
McAnally, Elizabeth Ann.
  Middle school general music : the best part of your day / Elizabeth Ann McAnally.
     p. cm.
  "Published in partnership with MENC : The National Association for Music Education."
  Includes bibliographical references.
  ISBN 978-1-60709-313-8 (cloth : alk. paper) — ISBN 978-1-60709-314-5 (pbk. : alk.
paper) — ISBN 978-1-60709-315-2 (electronic)
  1. School music—Instruction and study—Outlines, syllabi, etc. 2. School music—
Instruction and study—Handbooks, manuals, etc. I. MENC, the National Association for
Music Education (U.S.) II. National standards for music education. III. Title.
  MT10.M382 2009
  780.71'2—dc22   2009034484

♾ ™ The paper used in this publication meets the minimum requirements of American
National Standard for Information Sciences—Permanence of Paper for Printed Library
Materials, ANSI/NISO Z39.48-1992.

Printed in the United States of America

Contents

Preface

I distinctly remember the first moment I ever considered teaching in middle school. I was a junior in college, and apparently I had challenged my music education professor a few too many times. She looked at me and said, "Beth, you would make a very good middle school teacher." It did not seem, at the time, to be a compliment. My first thought was, "No way!"

After several years of teaching in an elementary school in a large urban area, I decided to apply for a transfer within the district to something closer to home. On my transfer request, I listed several schools in my neighborhood, including one middle school. Of course, that was the school with the first opening, and I was officially reassigned. When summer was over, I would teach middle school general music, becoming one of several music teachers serving a student body of over 1,200 adolescents. This time, my first thought was, "What have I done?"

It has now been more years than I care to admit, and I've discovered that my professor was right. Middle school is the best place for me. I teach general music classes and codirect a 175-voice choir. My days are a blur of classes, rehearsals, conferences with students, meetings with colleagues, and phone calls to parents. Although I am very busy, I am never bored.

And yet, the teaching assignment that has brought me so much fulfillment seems to provide unending dread for many of my fellow music teachers. If one were to take a survey of music educators to determine their idea of a "dream job," I imagine that middle school general music would probably be at the bottom of the list.

It is my belief that one contributing factor is a lack of attention to the challenges of teaching early adolescents. Many music educators who find themselves in middle school feel unprepared to teach this age. Student teaching assignments often include elementary and high school, but not middle-level experiences. Resources published for this age can be either too challenging or too immature.

Middle school music teachers are often left to navigate the minefield of changing voices and changing bodies alone.

For other music educators, middle school general music represents a distraction from their true passion of conducting instrumental and choral ensembles. As there are few middle schools with sufficient resources to allow for a full-time ensemble position, these teachers find the remainder of their roster filled with general music classes for which they are unprepared or in which they are uninterested.

Regardless of your circumstances, it is my hope that this book provides you with some ideas and strategies that are appropriate for middle-level students in general music classes. As is the case for many in-service teachers, I tend to focus on practice more than theory. Of course, every school presents unique challenges and benefits, so lessons may need to be modified to fit the needs of your students. For the sake of convenience, chapters are organized according to the National Standards for Music Education. It is not my intention to present one academic year of material, nor are the lessons in sequential order. Rather, this is more like a recipe book, where a teacher may pick and choose at will.

The purpose of this book is to share strategies that really work for middle school general music. My methods are decidedly eclectic in nature, and I make no claim to "expertise" in the field. My suggestions are not the only way, and probably not even the best way, but there is nothing in this book that I have not tested and refined in my own classroom with diverse groups of students. It is my sincere hope that the ideas presented here will be of use in your classroom, and will help you feel as I do—that middle school general music is the best part of your day.

I would like to express my sincere gratitude to Carolyn Tanner, my first music teacher, for starting me on this path so many years ago; to my husband and children for their constant support and patience during the preparation of this manuscript; and to my students and colleagues in the School District of Philadelphia for providing an endless source of inspiration.

Why Middle School General Music?

Teaching middle school general music is a bit like running a marathon—at the pace of a sprint. The weeks, months, and years can sometimes seem a blur of rushing here and there to meet the many responsibilities of a professional music educator. But every now and then, there are moments of absolute clarity, when we know that we've made a difference for a child.

There's the girl who was absent, late, or suspended from school nearly every day—unless she had music class. There's the boy who stuttered so badly that he wouldn't raise his hand to answer a question—unless it was in music class. There's the girl who introduced herself on the first day by asserting, "I don't sing!" but by the end of the term was asking, "Can we sing that song again?" There's the student with special needs who was so intrigued by a lesson on great classical-period composers that his holiday gift to the teacher was a music box that played a Beethoven melody.

As a middle school general music teacher, there are things I know and believe that, prior to this project, I'd never thought much about trying to prove with research or data. My professional life is staked on the claim that music is good for middle school students; it can help them cope with the myriad difficulties that confront kids at this age, and it can be a source of comfort throughout their lives. It can become an area of interest they didn't know they had, and may even provide direction for their future. It can help them see and understand their world in new ways.

In addition, it is my belief that middle school general music represents our last, best hope for convincing adolescents that they can be musical. For many, this will be the last music class they are required to take, and so it will be our last opportunity to provide sequential instruction to the entire student body. The students who participate in middle school band, choir, and orchestra already understand that music can be an important part of their lives, but what about the others? Our one remaining chance is general music class.

Unfortunately, we work in an educational climate that has undermined the place of the arts in school. According to a national survey published by the Center on Education Policy, 44 percent of the 349 representative districts reported that they had reduced the amount of time devoted to nontested subjects. As a matter of fact, the average instruction time per week for art *and* music in middle school was 167 minutes, which is less than all other subjects; the only activity receiving less time was lunch (2007).

So if we are already working with less time for music and, by extension, less money, why is middle school general music important enough to continue getting a piece of the pie? Why not use the time and money for programs that focus on students who are really interested in music? Why should this program be considered on the same level as band, choir, and orchestra?

If you're waiting for the well-used and well-intentioned argument that music improves standardized test scores, you won't find it here. I certainly do believe that music instruction helps create better students, and I do think that there are occasions when using that rationale is both logical and legitimate. However, for our purposes I'd like to take a look at data and professional literature that support what good middle school music teachers already know—that sequential instruction in music can help address the unique needs of young adolescents.

Let's start with the notion that music already has a place in the lives of *all* students, not just those who already play an instrument or sing in a choir. Adolescents are surrounded by it every day—on the radio and television, in restaurants, malls and video games. Their days are accompanied by an ever-present soundtrack of commercial jingles, Top 40 hits, and iPod playlists.

And let's not forget that music has been a part of the human condition for a very long time. An article published recently in *Nature* tells about the exciting discovery in southwestern Germany of fragments of a bone flute that are thought to be at least 35,000 years old (Conard, Malina, and Munzel, 2009). It has also been discovered that the locations of some cave paintings seem to correspond to areas within the caves that have the best acoustics (Whipps, 2008).

Ancient history aside, one has to wonder about the legitimacy of a school program that does not reach *all* students. What would we think of a middle school that offered mathematics or language arts instruction to only part of the student body? In an article for *General Music Today*, Timothy Gerber and Kevin Gerrity also express concern regarding this issue: "The total middle school music program *per se* is in jeopardy when its offerings do not reach every child—the remaining two-thirds of the school that do not elect music performance courses" (2007, 18). They go on to discuss the need for music educators to remind their administrators and colleagues about the place of music in the school curriculum: "We were not hired to teach only the talented few. We are there to teach everyone" (20).

If we can agree that music is important for all students, and that general music is the vehicle by which music instruction is delivered to students who have not chosen to participate in a performing ensemble, then we have begun to make an argument for the inclusion of general music classes in middle school. But what is it specifically about early adolescence that is so important for students, and why is it vital to provide music instruction during this period?

According to an article in *Middle School Journal*, significant changes in the prefrontal cortex occur during adolescence. "Though neuroscientists do not have a full understanding of why this occurs, the general conclusion is that adolescent brains go through a period of circuit refinement, pruning unused connections and strengthening more heavily used synapses" (Wilson and Horch 2002, 58). Essentially, the activities that our students engage in the most strengthen certain connections in that area of the brain, while connections that are not being used may be lost for good. The authors comment that "the saying 'use it or lose it' applies to brain growth during early adolescence" (58).

This idea is supported by Daniel J. Levitin, who says, "Our brains are developing and forming new connections at an explosive rate throughout adolescence, but this slows down substantially after our teenage years, the formative phase when our neural circuits become structured out of our experiences" (2006, 227). The implication for us is that students who are not receiving music instruction in middle school may be losing out on a critical opportunity.

Research conducted by the Philadelphia Education Fund and Johns Hopkins University identifies the middle school years as particularly crucial for overall school success. Researchers followed the progress of nearly 11,000 students who entered sixth grade in the School District of Philadelphia during the fall of 1996 up to the time of publication in 2005. They looked for three red-flag issues: failing grades in English or math, behavior issues, or less than 80 percent attendance. Only 10 percent of students with at least one red flag in sixth grade managed to graduate high school on time. And if that isn't frightening enough, nearly 32 percent of the students studied had at least one red flag (Mezzacappa, 2005). In other words, many middle school students exhibit issues that will likely interfere with later school success.

Now we've established that the middle school years are a turning point. Students who receive strong instruction in a particular subject during adolescence are strengthening the connections in the brain that support that activity. And students who find success in middle school have a greater chance for success in high school. So what role can and should music play in meeting the needs of our students? Is there something special about music that reaches them in a way that other disciplines cannot?

Let's think back for a moment to our own middle school years. No, don't cringe—I'm not referring to peer pressure, unfortunate fashion choices, or hormonally induced temper tantrums. I'm thinking about music, and the first musical choices we likely made on our own, rather than having the choices made for us by our parents. For many of us, it was the first time that we purchased recordings with our own money (remember those eight-track tapes?) or chose to listen to favorite radio stations in our bedrooms instead of joining family activities. Our musical preferences became part of the way we expressed our emerging self-identities. We liked songs that spoke to us, and helped us speak for ourselves. Chances are good that we remember a lot of those songs, and that hearing them again brings back startlingly vivid memories. We probably remember more about the music we liked in adolescence than the facts we were taught in class.

All these things are true for our students, too. As Gerber and Gerrity tell us, "Finding meaning in one's life begins in earnest in middle school. Music often plays a central role in that search for personal understanding" (2007, 22). Levitin mentions that "music and musical preferences become a mark of personal and group identity and of distinction" (2006, 226).

Our students are already listening to music and developing their own preferences. Do we really want to leave our students solely in the hands of a commercially driven popular-music industry? Doesn't it seem better to introduce our students to a whole world full of vibrant music (yes, including popular music) from many cultures and time periods? Middle school general music class may be the only opportunity for some students to interact with that larger musical world.

We also know, from our own experiences and from observing the experiences of our students, that middle school can be a turbulent, frightening time. Poverty, abuse, depression, and other issues affect many students. How might music instruction benefit those considered to be "at risk"? Some researchers feel that music can affect stress levels and the immune system. It is thought that music may affect heart rate and antibody levels, as well as perhaps lowering the level of cortisol, a hormone involved in feelings of stress (Jensen, 2001). In light of our increasingly high-pressure standardized testing, it is also important to note that the arts can keep students engaged in school: "As one refuge for at-risk students with test anxiety, the arts themselves often keep young people in school" (Gerber and Gerrity, 2007, 20).

Now it seems that we have a clearer picture. Music instruction should be for all students, and general music should be offered to serve the needs of those uninterested in performing ensembles. The middle school years are a particularly important time, when the choices made for and by students have far-reaching implications. And music can speak to adolescents in a poignant and memorable way. Taken together, these points make a strong case for middle school general music.

Let's also take time to consider what we hope to accomplish through our general music program. Should our priority be to create a discerning audience, promote music literacy, or foster multicultural awareness? Do we want proficient singers, pianists, guitar players? Should students learn how to utilize technology while composing and arranging? And what if my answer is different from your answer, or the answers of our colleagues?

Luckily, much of this work has already been done for us. The National Standards for Arts Education (see Appendix A), published in 1994 and developed collaboratively by respected arts educators, lists clear and challenging standards to guide us in our planning. Standards are stated in terms of observable skills with age-appropriate benchmarks. The National Standards make it easy to evaluate our programs for balance and depth, while still leaving room for the strengths and interests of individual teachers to flourish. Although state standards may vary in their format and complexity, the National Standards have provided a unifying vision for music educators around the country.

But just for a moment, let's also think a little further ahead—instead of focusing solely on what our students should know and be able to do by the end of the school year, let's think about what we hope they can do twenty years from now, when their middle school days have long since faded into memory. When nagged into attending an orchestra performance by a spouse, will they be able to find meaning in the music? When attending a party, will they mumble "Happy Birthday," hoping that no one will hear them sing? Will there be a piano or guitar in their homes? Will their musical tastes be eclectic, one-dimensional, or nonexistent? Will they volunteer for a church choir or community theater? Will they encourage their own children to participate in music activities?

Maybe our students will come back to visit us and we can ask those questions. But for now, let's continue to plant seeds that have the greatest possible chance to flourish, no matter where they might choose to grow.

CHAPTER 1

National Standard 1

National Standard 1: Singing, alone and with others, a varied repertoire of music.

(Consortium of National Arts
Education Associations, 1994, 42)

If there's one thing that a middle school general music teacher knows, it's that it can be very difficult to get kids to sing. Who among us, after the most brilliant cue and the most enthusiastic "Ready, sing!" hasn't been faced with an overwhelming wall of silence? A singing activity in general music can be met with indifference, lethargy, orneriness, or downright hostility from even the best of classes.

So, why bother? There are so many other battles to fight—why pick this one? It's so much easier to convince students to play piano, guitar, or other instruments; is it really that important that they sing, too?

It is my belief that singing is a crucial component of a general music program. Pianos and guitars are not present in every home, and instrumental lessons are not a part of all families' weekly routine. The only instrument we can be assured that our students will possess now and for a lifetime is the voice. Without careful handling, our students will grow to be adults who won't sing in the church choir, who avoid karaoke like the plague, and who will only sing in the shower if no one else is home.

If you're looking for an extended treatise on training the adolescent voice, there are any number of available resources written by vocal experts. However, in this chapter we will explore a few strategies that encourage middle school students to sing in the first place. After all, vocal training cannot occur without participation.

1

Before we begin, just a word about priorities. In my general music classroom, the primary goal during singing activities is to foster a love of singing. For some students, this will be the end of formal music education, so it is the last chance to create students (and, later, adults) who are comfortable using their singing voices and enjoy doing so. Of course, secondary goals for singing activities include good breath control, proper diction, part-singing, and an appreciation for a variety of song styles. However, unlike in the choral-performance program, if a few of the niceties are placed temporarily on the back burner in general music for the sake of a fun singing experience, I for one do not consider that wasted time.

The following are some strategies for cultivating a love of singing:

Give "The Speech." Do you remember what it feels like to hope the teacher won't call on you, even when you know the answer? How much worse would it be to be called on by the music teacher to sing all by yourself? (If my teacher had done that to me, I would probably never have sung in public again.) To avoid such a disaster for my students, I have prepared "The Speech." Here's how it goes: "I promise I will never, never, never make you sing a solo. You will never be asked to sing by yourself for a grade. However, we will sing as a group, and you will be graded for participation." The key to successful use of the Speech is to repeat it often, especially after a less-than-enthusiastic response to a new song. By the end of the semester, most of my students can repeat "The Speech" verbatim.

Establish a safety net. An adolescent's greatest fear is to be laughed at, so deal with that bad habit right away. Whether the class is laughing at a student, the teacher, or the song, be serious and firm in your reminder that no one is to be treated disrespectfully. Participation in singing activities is much more likely when students feel sure that you will not allow them to be objects of ridicule.

Present a broad repertoire. Any middle school class of thirty students represents at least forty different musical preferences. So how can a teacher choose a song that the whole class will like? Well, you can't, but there are some ways to improve your success rate.

Try to use a variety of music, so if a student doesn't like this week's song, chances are he or she may like next week's. Also, choose lyrics to which students can relate; songs about love are surprisingly popular, and goofy songs that appeal to the middle school sense of humor are usually a safe bet. Adolescents tend to enjoy a fast tempo with lots of percussion—when asked why they like a particular song, a typical response is "I like the beat."

You may wish to avoid songs that are currently trendy, as they often go out of style very quickly. Songs from the 1950s and 1960s get a lot of airtime in my room, as do Broadway tunes and songs from movie soundtracks. Students will often surprise us, so do take a risk every now and then. Sometimes it's possible to appeal to the middle school sense of orneriness by introducing a song by saying, "I'm not sure if you're going to like this one."

Be attentive to range. The adolescent male vocal change can be very problematic when planning singing activities, especially since this change occurs at different times for different students. It is very likely that you will have both changed and unchanged voices in the same class, even up through eighth grade. It can be very helpful to teach the boys how to choose the octave that best fits, and to remind them that they may need to choose differently on another day. Then, look for songs that can be sung easily at either octave.

For the younger grades, it helps to aim for working in, or close to, the key of F major, with most of a song using a range of about a perfect fifth. The octave above middle C is not too high, and the octave below middle C works well for the cambiata voice. In the older grades, the keys of C or D seem to work best, and a somewhat wider range is feasible. Boys with changed voices are very happy at C or D below middle C, while the girls are content from middle C to third-space C.

Emphasize posture. Student seating in some music rooms consists of desks with book rests underneath the seats—bad news for singing, as the book rests are usually used as foot rests. When it's time to sing, insist on both feet flat on the floor, and backs straight. It takes much repetition to successfully form the habit of good posture, but the improved sound makes it well worth the time. A daily reminder about proper posture for singing also serves as an obvious cue that singing is a special activity.

Know when to stop. One of the best things to hear in the general music room is "Can we sing it again?" This is a cue to move on to something else by saying, "Let's sing it again tomorrow." The students now have something to look forward to, and they may think that they have successfully manipulated their teacher into changing tomorrow's plans. Most likely, the song is already planned for the next day, but things will go more smoothly if the students think that an activity was their idea!

Divide and conquer. When confronted with singing that lacks energy, it can be helpful to shake things up a bit. Although whole-group singing is often most appropriate, this is the time to divide the class into two or three parts. Alternate which group sings the verse, and have the whole class join in on the refrain. Or have one section sing while the other conducts, and then exchange jobs at the next verse. Choose two students to be the judges, and ask them to decide which group has the best posture, best diction, or best energy while singing; the winning section chooses the next song. It's usually best to start and finish with whole-group singing; students have a chance to warm up together, and everyone can enjoy the reenergized sound at the end.

Utilize student leadership. Adolescents are not naturally responsive to authority, unless it is their own. Choose a volunteer to conduct, and make a big deal of sitting and singing with the group. Appoint captains to distribute and collect books, place a student in charge of the CD player, or find a page turner to help you at the piano. Middle school students like to help as much as their younger counterparts—they would just rather be called "leaders" than "helpers."

Be creative. There are lots of ways to have students sing without fully realizing that's what they're doing. When students are having trouble learning a new song on the piano or resonator bells, it can be helpful to have them sing letter names while playing. In preparation for a listening activity, sing the motive or theme on a neutral syllable. Students can sing songs written by the composer they're studying, and songs from different cultures. Women's History Month, African American History Month, the anniversary of the penning of "The Star-Spangled Banner," and even the principal's birthday provide logical song choices. Invaluable learning connections are being made, and if the students' singing repertoire just happens to expand, so much the better. (In other words, if you don't announce, "This is a singing activity!" the students may not really notice that they're singing.)

Ask for their opinions. Giving students an opportunity to express their opinions appropriately is a useful tool. Try playing two recordings of the same song, and ask them to vote on which arrangement they like better. Or help students create their own arrangement by determining tempo, dynamics, voicing, and instrumentation. When there are a few minutes to spare at the end of class, allow students to make a list of page numbers of songs they would like to learn. You can even ask students their opinion of a particular song, but only after they have finished learning it!

Sing in original languages. When a song from another culture is used in a basal music series, an English version is often included. In order to make the English words fit the song's melody, the meaning of the original lyrics may be changed, sometimes drastically. For this reason, use the original language whenever possible. It takes encouragement for students to feel comfortable singing in a different language, but they become more aware of the wide world of music and culture that exists around them.

Use a moderate volume for accompaniment. Here's one of those subtle things that can make a big difference. If the volume of the accompaniment is too loud, the students can't hear themselves—they may have trouble matching pitch, or may stop singing altogether, thinking that no one will notice. If the volume is too soft, the students may be afraid that everyone can hear them, so they sing very softly or not at all. Aim for somewhere in the middle.

Remember that yelling is not singing. Middle school singers are creatures of extremes—left to their own devices, they will either whisper or shout instead of using their singing voices. Try to avoid asking students to sing louder, as yelling is the inevitable result. Instead, ask for more energy. Just because they yell in the hallways doesn't mean you should accept it in the music room.

Don't forget your pom-poms! Sometimes it seems that our job is to be more of a cheerleader than a vocal coach, and if silly encouragement distracts the students from their own self-consciousness, so much the better. Plan to lead by example, and sing with the students in a good, strong voice.

Whether your students admit it or not, they just might find that they actually like to sing. Thanks to your hard work supporting their growing musicianship, the songs you've taught them may last a lifetime. Before we know it, the world will be filled with adults who know all the words to "The Star-Spangled Banner," are the first to volunteer on karaoke night, and who entertain their grandchildren with stories that start with "That reminds me of a song . . ."

CHAPTER 2

National Standard 2

National Standard 2: Performing on instruments, alone and with others, a varied repertoire of music.

(Consortium of National Arts
Education Associations, 1994, 42)

Does this sound familiar to you? You step out of the music room for a moment, and when you return, somebody is playing around on the piano. Loudly. It might not even be a student that you know, and it's entirely possible that said student hasn't the first idea how to play a recognizable melody. Or even a pleasant one. And this child will probably not be very happy to be asked to stop.

As discussed in the last chapter, there are many reasons why singing in general music class is very important, despite the motivational challenges that may ensue. However, what our students really want to do is learn how to play an instrument. They may not even be very picky about which one—they just want to play. Whether it's rhythm sticks, recorder, guitar, resonator bells, or piano, when our students have instruments in their hands, it seems that they are instantly motivated to participate. They may come back to visit years later, and head straight to the piano to see if they still know a song they learned in middle school general music!

In addition to the motivational benefits, spending time on National Standard 2 may yield other rewards as well. When a parent asks the usual end-of-day question, "What did you do in school today?" the middle school child who ordinarily replies, "Nothing," may actually talk about the song he or she learned to play in music class. And administrators who see students playing instruments usually leave with the feeling that substantial learning has taken place. "Wow, you should hear what Mrs. Rivera's students are doing in music. They can really play the [insert name of instrument here]."

The nice part about playing instruments with middle school students is that these activities provide opportunities to address other National Standards at the same time, *without the students even realizing it*. When learning to play a song, students will need to read the notation, sing the letter names or lyrics, listen to themselves and other players, evaluate their own performance, and learn about the composer, culture, or time period. They may think they are just learning to play a song on the bells; little do they know that they've covered nearly all the National Standards in one activity.

Now that I've mentioned the benefits of playing instruments in general music class, I would be remiss if I didn't bring up the challenges. For one thing, middle school kids plus instruments equals noise. Sometimes lots and lots of noise. After all, there's a reason why our students make so many mistakes on the rests—they don't like to be quiet! In addition, some instruments are expensive and require storage room; not every school has that kind of money or space to invest in the general music program. The purpose of this chapter is to address these concerns by providing some tips about playing instruments with middle school students, along with a few activities for classroom percussion and a discussion about how to plan activities when you don't have an instrument for every child.

Tips for Instrumental Activities

Tip #1: Teach the "rest position" before teaching how to play a single note. It will save countless migraines if your students know how to hold an instrument without making a sound. As I remind my students, "This is not 'noise class.' You already know how to make noise. This is music class."

Tip #2: They don't have to all play at the same time. As a matter of fact, it's better if they don't. If you have enough instruments for one quarter to one third of the class to play together, you have enough instruments. In order for everyone to have a turn, you have a built-in reason to repeat the song three or four times.

Tip #3: Plan several ways to vary the activity. After the first group of players has had a turn, the next group can play a little bit faster. Or add a simple rhythm ostinato for the rest of the class to clap. Add a repeat, a coda, or an introduction. Add harmony, or play in canon, or play the whole thing backward. Each time the activity repeats, change things a little bit so that everyone has to pay attention and the difficulty level gradually increases.

Tip #4: Homemade instruments and "found sounds" are still instruments. If you don't have a lot of instruments to work with, enlist the help of your students to create some. It could be a homework assignment for each student to bring in an object that makes a sound. (Be sure to discuss appropriate and inappropriate things to bring to school.) Or assign a "make your own instrument" project, and challenge students to create instruments that have more than one source of vibration.

Tip #5: Teach instrument parts from notation. Whether it's a four-beat ostinato or a sixteen-measure melody, keep putting notation in front of your students. They need to learn to connect symbol and sound, and that takes time and repetition. Take advantage of highly motivational activities like playing instruments to reinforce notation skills.

Tip #6: Encourage kids to sing while they play. A student who refuses to participate during a singing activity might be willing to sing letter names while playing the piano. Developing the singing voice without placing overt emphasis on it is a very effective strategy for teaching adolescents. In addition, students tend to play instrumental parts more accurately and with a steadier beat when they sing along. Just don't compliment their singing right now; they'd rather not know that they're doing it.

Tip #7: Play instruments at the end of the lesson. If you need your students to be focused and able to listen carefully to important material, it will be easier to accomplish this if they didn't just finish playing boomwhackers and conga drums.

Tip #8: Leave time at the end of the activity for students to help put the instruments away. Do you really have time to stack up fifteen coffee can maracas, count thirty pairs of mallets, or turn off all the keyboards before the next class arrives? Of course not, and helping your students develop a sense of responsibility will be time well spent.

Activities for Classroom Percussion Instruments

Note: The term "classroom percussion instruments" is used very loosely here, referring to those small, reasonably priced instruments that are not usually a main part of school instrumental programs. So maracas, hand drums, triangles, and so forth would be included, while flute, timpani, trombone, and violin would not.

Classroom percussion instruments provide a wonderful opportunity to put a whole world of instruments into the hands of your students. They can see a Bolivian goat-hoof shaker, a Peruvian rainstick, a Tibetan singing bowl, an African gourd shekere, and a Vietnamese frog guiro in one class period. Whenever possible, try to acquire authentic native instruments, rather than factory-made reproductions. These instruments can be found in several major music retail catalogs, as well as in the exhibit halls of many MENC national, divisional, and state conferences.

Once you have developed a bit of a collection, you might challenge your students to consider questions like these: What country or culture does the instrument come from? From what materials is the instrument made? Can these materials be easily found in this culture, or do they need to be imported? Do you see any similarities between instruments from different cultures, countries, or continents? Could the instrument be handmade, or is it usually constructed in a factory? What is the source of the instrument's vibration? How many different sounds can be created with this instrument?

In addition to providing an opportunity to learn about music from many cultures, classroom percussion instruments can be used to enhance other activities without much added preparation or additional lesson time. Here are a few ideas to try:

- Help students create a short ostinato to play during the instrumental bridge of a song they have learned to sing.
- Choose an instrument for students to play on the strong beat of each measure and a contrasting instrument to play on the weak beat(s). Use this activity to illustrate the difference between duple and triple meter.
- Use pitched percussion such as resonator bells or boomwhackers to play chord roots along with a recording of twelve-bar blues or another repeated chord progression.
- Choose students to play a four- or eight-beat rhythm on a classroom instrument while the rest of the class takes rhythm dictation.

Other uses for classroom instruments can be found in the chapters about improvisation and composition, so keep reading!

A good way to help students learn to perform rhythms independently is to create interlocking rhythm patterns. It works with short, simple rhythms as well as longer, more complex ones, and can also be done with rhythms composed by students. This example will use fairly basic rhythms; so, if necessary, modify the activity to fit the needs of your students.

Before class begins, create three rhythms that are two measures in length, using quarter notes, quarter rests, and eighth-note pairs, and end each rhythm with a repeat sign. Write them on a large piece of chart paper, and label the rhythms A, B, and C. Post the chart paper where everyone can see it clearly.

The first task is to be sure that all students can clap the rhythms correctly and independently. Once that has been achieved, divide the class into three parts—A, B, and C. Be sure that each group can clap their assigned rhythm without help. A word of warning: if a rhythm has a few quarter rests in it, an unintended accelerando may occur. Counting out loud can help avoid that common pitfall. It also helps to ask students to clap lightly; the louder the dynamics, the faster the tempo.

Now the students are ready to put the rhythms together. Begin with the A section, and have students clap it at a steady tempo, repeating continuously until told to stop. When the A section is secure, have the B section join in, and then the C section. The three rhythms form an interlocking pattern.

Next, help the students choose a different instrument for each section. Hand out enough instruments for about four or five students from each part to be playing at one time. Students who are awaiting a turn should clap their part lightly. Repeat the activity several times, passing the instruments to different students each time. To keep students interested, add the parts in a different order, have them stop at different times, or add a crescendo or decrescendo. You might also use the three sections to create a rondo.

Activities with Limited Instruments

Of course, it's hard to help your students meet the challenge of this National Standard without instruments to play. For the readers who have access to twenty-five guitars or a full keyboard lab, congratulations are due to both you and your school district for allocating these resources to your young musicians. For those who teach with funding challenges or an unsupportive budgetary process, the rest of the chapter is for you. The next section will describe a teaching sequence that can be used to teach basic piano skills. These strategies could also apply to other instruments; as always, modify them to fit your own situation.

For this example, imagine a classroom with three pianos and more than thirty students at a time. Although it may seem like an insurmountable challenge, it is quite possible and even rewarding to teach piano in these circumstances. In addition to these instruments, let's add thirty plastic, two-octave "practice keyboards" that can be purchased from a music supply catalog. (A photocopied keyboard chart is an acceptable second choice, but its two-dimensional nature can be problematic.) A practice keyboard and a copy of the notation for the song are distributed to students at the beginning of each lesson. The steps outlined below will illustrate how an entire class might be able to play a song when only these few instruments are available.

STEP 1

Help students learn the song from notation, using the strategies with which they are most familiar. You might have them clap the rhythm, sing the letter names, analyze the melodic contour, or interpret important symbols such as repeat signs and first and second endings.

STEP 2

Using the practice keyboards, ask students to "play" through the song. Depending on the complexity and length of the piece, it may be necessary to teach smaller segments and then combine them when the students are ready. Be sure to move around the room to check for correct hand position and fingering, and to provide guidance where needed.

STEP 3

Choose six students to take a turn at the instruments, assigning two students to each piano. (To avoid uncomfortable situations, it is wise to pair girls with girls and boys with boys, especially if they are going to share a piano bench.) Establish the tempo by counting out a measure or two, and then have the students play the song together. Students who are still at their seats are expected to follow the same directions at their practice keyboards.

STEP 4

Repeat the previous step four more times, until all students have had a turn. To keep everyone engaged in the activity, change the directions slightly for each group. Switch from one hand to the other, increase the tempo, or add dynamics. If students were directed to sing the letter names while one group took a turn, have them count aloud for the next group.

Just like in any activity with young adolescents, it is important to keep a pace that will allow everyone to have a turn before the class exhausts its attention span. If time is not sufficient to allow all students to play, consider a different activity, or assure the students who did not have a turn that they will be chosen first at the beginning of the next lesson.

You may be wondering if it is really possible for thirty middle school students to be successful at an activity that requires so much patience. In my experience, if students are *taught* the expectations, feel that the music is neither too easy nor too hard, and can see that everyone in the class is given a chance, they usually rise to the challenge. It is also helpful to intersperse these lessons with other activities in which the whole class participates simultaneously.

Whether you must use letter grades, number grades, or something else entirely, how should progress toward meeting this standard be assessed? Is it fair to compare a student who has never played piano before to a student who has received several years of private instruction? What exactly are we assessing, and who has time to observe all these kids, anyway?

First, it is quite reasonable to consider participation as part of a grade. When students participate fully in an instrumental activity, they are almost certainly improving their skills in playing that instrument. Also, it's not easy for adolescents to try something new in such a public forum, so simply overcoming their natural fear of failure is no small accomplishment. When students feel that their teacher is more interested in noticing their effort than their mistakes, they can move past their discomfort and concentrate on mastering the musical challenge.

Assessment

As for the assessment of specific skills, a tiered assessment given to students individually can be very effective. In this type of evaluation, students are asked to prepare for a performance test, and they are given a list of songs with a varying degree of technical complexity from which to choose. In order to earn the highest grade, the most difficult option is required. The least difficult option earns a lower, yet still very respectable, score. A rubric or list of criteria is also explained beforehand, and can include expectations about technique, tempo, and rhythmic and melodic accuracy. When the performance test is given, students are assessed individually while their classmates are engaged in an independent activity. This helps to reduce the anxiety many students feel when asked to perform alone.

This approach is admittedly quite time consuming. You might also try keeping a checklist of the specific skills you are assessing, and observe a few students each lesson. A self-evaluation form for students to complete at the beginning and end of the term could also be helpful.

Despite the logistical challenges, playing instruments with students is a very meaningful and rewarding part of a middle school general music program. Instrumental activities hold much inherent motivational value, and can also address other National Standards simultaneously. Before you know it, students will be asking for extra practice time before and after school, volunteering to play their own compositions for the class, and convincing their parents to buy instruments as holiday presents. And the next time you return to the music room to find a student playing the piano, you may be pleasantly surprised by what you hear!

CHAPTER 3

National Standard 3

National Standard 3: Improvising melodies, variations, and accompaniments.

(Consortium of National Arts
Education Associations, 1994, 43)

For many musicians, there is nothing more frightening than improvisation. Despite a centuries-long tradition of improvisation, classically trained musicians are usually taught only to play the notes on the page. We have learned to read notation quickly and accurately, and we concern ourselves primarily with the importance of replicating the composer's intentions. Improvisation is viewed to be a mysterious skill that is granted to the lucky few at birth; in other words, either you have it or you don't. Those who have been convinced that they are among the "have-nots" develop a different skill—the ability to avoid improvisation at all costs. Many won't improvise even when there's no one else around to hear.

However, in spite of our claims to the contrary, we improvise every day. For example, we may improvise a recipe, a new route to work, or a solution to a household plumbing problem. Similarly, the lessons we teach are also strongly rooted in improvisation. We learn to quickly assess the prior knowledge and skills of our students, and then use our experience to improvise the most effective method to help students meet the lesson's objective. We resist and resent curricula that include scripted lessons because we don't want to be restricted—we want to improvise.

Interestingly enough, it seems that the discomfort felt by adults about improvisation is a learned behavior. Even casual observation of children at play will yield many examples of improvisation that occur naturally, both musical and otherwise. From the two-year-old who makes up a story to match the pictures in a book to the middle-schooler who improvises complex rhythms and melodies on a keyboard, children have not yet learned that improvisation is something to be feared.

Unfortunately, National Standard 3 is probably the one that receives the least attention in our music-education programs. We plan many activities that teach music notation (not a topic to which students gravitate naturally), but neglect improvisation because we've "run out of time." Because we feel uncomfortable, we avoid improvisation in the classroom, and so our students miss out on the opportunity to develop a skill that they enjoy.

This chapter will include activities that encourage improvisation in the middle school general music classroom, as well as tips for creating a safe environment for students. If you wish, they can be used to build upon and reinforce the learning of other National Standards. Many are quite short, and can easily be fit into a few minutes at the beginning or end of a lesson, or used to fill those troublesome transition points. After trying one or two of these ideas, you are likely to find your own ways to include improvisation in your general music program. These activities are designed to put even the most improvisation-phobic at ease, so relax and enjoy!

Getting Started

- Before asking your students to take a musical risk, be sure that the environment you've created in your classroom is very supportive. Never allow students to laugh at each other, and teach them how to make descriptive comments ("I noticed that Julia used lots of eighth notes during her turn"). Students will learn to fear improvisation if they are ridiculed by their peers.
- Teacher comments following student improvisation should also be descriptive, not evaluative. For example, say, "Did you notice how Hai decided to end on C with a whole note?" rather than "Hai's improvisation was the only one that sounded complete!"
- Our students are very accustomed to looking for one right answer, so we will need to help them understand that there are many correct responses in improvisation. At first, students may ask, "Is that right?" as soon as they finish. Remind them often that the only wrong answer is no answer at all.
- Be careful with the spotlight. Some students only feel truly safe with improvisation when they think no one is listening. Avoid asking individual students to perform lengthy improvisations in front of the class until they are very, very comfortable, and even then do so only on an optional, volunteer basis. Our goal is to teach students to love improvisation, not dread it.
- If you are one of the many musicians who are inexperienced in improvisation, prepare carefully for these lessons and present a confident image to the class.

If you act uncomfortable, reluctant, or self-conscious, your students will do the same.

- Make your first activities very short. After all, clapping four beats is much less intimidating than playing twelve-bar blues on the piano. When students feel confident with shorter activities, gradually increase the length.
- Also consider making your first activities fairly simple. You might try rhythm improvisation first, and later add melody. Or limit students to a few choices in the beginning (quarter notes and eighth notes before adding sixteenth notes and syncopation). As the class becomes accustomed to improvisation, add complexity.
- Despite the guidelines suggested above, don't be afraid to try an "anything goes" activity. The structure described in the previous tips is comforting for some, but frustrating for others. For those students, the effort it takes to remember the imposed limitations interrupts the natural flow of their improvisation. In such circumstances, our primary job is to get out of the way and let them explore their musical ideas.
- Incorporate improvisation into other lessons. For example, if your students are learning to take rhythmic dictation, ask for a volunteer to improvise an example for the class to notate. Or if the group is listening to Mozart's variations on "Ah vous dirai-je, Maman," encourage students to improvise their own variations to the familiar "Twinkle, Twinkle" melody. And many students will naturally begin a composition project by improvising; all you have to do is give them a label for what they are already doing.

Call-and-Response Activities

These ideas work well in conjunction with lessons that teach the concept of call-and-response. Extension activities might include listening to folk music from different cultures, as well as performances by jazz legends. Song selections from basal music series that include call-and-response would further reinforce the theme.

TEACHER / WHOLE CLASS, THEN
TEACHER / INDIVIDUAL STUDENT

After explaining or reviewing the meaning of call-and-response, tell students that they will have the opportunity to improvise a response after you improvise a call. The parameters are simple: each call and each response will be a clapped rhythm that is two measures long, four beats per measure. For the first few tries, you clap the call, and all the students improvise the response at the same time. Of course, this yields a rather chaotic result, but each student is free to create his or her own rhythm without any fear of judgment from peers. It is helpful to count the beats aloud to keep everyone together.

After everyone has had a few chances to experiment, it is time to allow individual students to improvise the response by themselves. Again, you improvise a two-measure rhythm; but this time, students are selected randomly to improvise a two-measure response. As you clap your part, move around the room, stopping next to the student who will have the next turn—making sure to stop a few beats ahead so the student has a moment to get ready. This is a fairly low-pressure activity, as the students only have to improvise eight beats and are selected quickly, leaving very little time for them to get nervous.

There are a number of variations to this activity that can be used to keep students interested, and to support other objectives. For example, rhythm improvisation can be replaced with melodic improvisation using resonator bells, keyboards, or whatever you happen to have available. To make the results musically pleasing, you can select the pitches students are permitted to include in their improvisation. You might use pentatonic, major, minor, or blues scales. Also, student leadership can be fostered by choosing a volunteer to improvise the call in place of the teacher. You could also have students work in pairs to improvise a call-and-response pattern. Another way to extend the activity is to make each improvisation longer by increasing to four or eight measures. To keep your students on their toes, never do the activity the same way twice.

STUDENT/STUDENT

To use this "improvisation relay" you will need a little bit of space, about eight volunteers to start, and two sets of simple percussion instruments, such as rhythm sticks, woodblocks, or hand drums. Divide the volunteers evenly, and place them in two relay lines, with the first people in line facing each other and the others standing directly behind them.

The students at the front of the lines take turns improvising a two-measure rhythm. It usually works best to have each person take two turns, or, in other words, to have two sets of call-and-response. When a student's turn is complete, he or she quickly hands the instrument to the next person in line, so that the chain of call-and-response is not broken. The person who has just finished may return to his or her seat or go to the back of the line to await another turn. Students from the class may join the back of a line whenever a spot opens up. It is fun to see how long the improvisation can continue without pause.

If you wish to use melodic instead of rhythmic improvisation, place two desks or small tables at the front of each line, with a keyboard or set of resonator bells atop each desk. In this variation, the students take turns improvising a melody of two or four measures. It will be important to designate which line plays the call and which line plays the response, and show students how to select the ending note to make their melodies sound incomplete or complete.

Activities That Include Both Composition and Improvisation

Improvisation and composition often go hand in hand. Many composers use improvisation to experiment with musical ideas before committing them to paper. Others leave space within compositions for improvisation to occur. And for some of our students, composition and improvisation are so closely related as to be essentially two sides of the same creative coin. These activities are designed to include both composition and improvisation, in order to provide structure for beginning improvisers and a safety net for students who lack confidence.

The primary reason for including composition and improvisation in the same activity is that it helps minimize the complexity of the task. After all, it is not easy for young musicians to juggle rhythm, melody, meter, form, dynamics, articulation, and tempo at the same time. Composing some of the musical ideas ahead of time essentially reduces the number of variables to consider while improvising. In addition, if the composition portion is accomplished as a class, the teacher has the opportunity to guide the students through a portion of the creative process. When the composed portion of the music is written down, the reading and notating of music is also reinforced.

COMPOSE THE CALL, IMPROVISE THE RESPONSE

Actually a variation on some of the call-and-response improvisations described previously, this activity involves the class composing a call and notating it on the chalkboard or chart paper. Instead of the teacher improvising the call, the class performs the composed call together between individual improvisations. This is a good way to encourage participation from the whole group, reducing the potential classroom-management issues that can occur when students don't have enough to do.

COMPOSE THE RHYTHM, IMPROVISE THE MELODY

To prepare for this activity, you will need to think about the comfort level and experience of your students in melodic improvisation. If your class has done a lot of improvisation or if they are very familiar with playing instruments, you might decide not to impose limitations about which pitches may be used. However, if your class is not as comfortable, you might limit the pitches to three to five. Resonator bells or Orff instruments work well for this activity because the selected pitches can be set up ahead of time.

To begin, you will guide your class as they compose a four- or eight-measure rhythm and notate it on a chalkboard or chart paper. When you are sure that everyone can clap or tap the rhythm accurately with a steady tempo, you are ready to add melody. One easy way is to prepare two sets of bells, and have a few volunteers stand in lines in front of them. When one student is finished improvising a melody to the composed rhythm, the person at the next set of bells takes a turn, while the first line moves forward. To keep the whole class involved, other students may clap the rhythm or perform it on classroom percussion instruments during the improvisations.

You may find that sometimes the composed rhythm will "evolve" slightly as more and more students take their turns improvising a melody. For example, quarter notes may become eighth-note pairs, and quarter rests may become quarter notes. If it seems appropriate, you may stop the improvisations to correct the rhythm; but if that would interrupt the students' creative flow, wait until all the volunteers have finished their turns. Then you might say, "I noticed that our rhythm changed slightly in the middle of the activity. Can anyone tell me where the change was? Which way do we like better? Why do you think the change happened?"

COMPOSE THE MELODY, IMPROVISE THE RHYTHM

This activity can be set up in much the same way as the previous one, only this time the class will choose the melody notes, and individuals will create their own rhythms for them. Determine ahead of time how many beats will be played on each note; two or four work nicely. It also works to use the chord roots for a repeated chord progression, such as the I–vi–IV–V7 progression used in songs like "Those Magic Changes" or the chord progressions used in familiar tunes such as the Pachelbel Canon or the Tallis Canon. As long as you stay in the same key, the improvisations could be performed along with a recording of a song that uses that chord progression.

COMPOSE THE CHORD PROGRESSION, IMPROVISE THE MELODY AND RHYTHM

A more advanced improvisation challenge, this requires that students understand how to quickly find the notes in a particular chord, and that they be able to easily move from one chord to another. It can be played on piano, resonator bells, or other pitched percussion instruments. If you wish to make the challenge more approachable, you might pull the appropriate resonator bells from the case, and set them up in chord groups. A shorter chord progression would be a good idea here! To keep the rest of your class involved, other students might play the chord roots as whole notes or half notes on the piano, bells, or even boomwhackers while volunteers improvise the melody and rhythm.

Other Improvisation Activities

Loosely speaking, anytime your students have the opportunity to create musical sounds on the spot, improvisation is occurring. The level of complexity and the length of the improvisation certainly do not have to meet professional standards in order for the activity to be useful and exciting for the class. Below are a few other ideas to try.

IMPROVISE TO CREATE A MOOD

To help students discover how a composer manipulates the elements of music to create a particular mood, allow your students to explore the range of sounds that can be produced by classroom instruments or found sounds. Ask your students to brainstorm a list of emotions or moods, and write them down on the chalkboard or chart paper. Distribute instruments and/or found-sound sources. As you call out a word from the list, students improvise with their instrument in a way that creates that particular mood or emotion. You can do this with all students at once, or perhaps have half the class improvise while the other half writes down a short description of what they heard. Be sure to plan for a follow-up discussion: "At what tempo did our musicians play? How did the dynamics make us think of that emotion? Was our improvisation successful in creating that mood?"

IMPROVISE AN ACCOMPANIMENT TO A SONG

This activity can be used to add excitement to a song that your class already knows well. Distribute classroom percussion instruments to five to ten students, and encourage them to improvise an accompaniment while the rest of the class sings. If you rotate the instruments to several other groups of students, your class may be more willing to try the song more than once in a class period.

IMPROVISE AN ENDING OR REPEATED PHRASE IN A SONG

For advanced improvisers and/or particularly brave students, vocal improvisation is another logical step in the process. However, for some middle school students, this is a very risky activity. Don't try this idea until you are absolutely sure that your class has learned how to be supportive of improvisation.

Some songs, such as "Go Down Moses," have a repeated phrase or a common ending for each verse. When students are very familiar with the song and can sing it well, ask for volunteers to create their own melody for the repeated phrase. Be prepared to demonstrate; if you act uncomfortable, your students will be also. Designate a different student for the selected phrase on each verse, and have the whole class perform the rest of the song. For an activity like this one, only use volunteers and never require that students improvise. Some students may never volunteer to improvise vocally in front of their peers, but for all we know, that's what they'll be singing in the shower the next morning.

Improvisation in the middle school general music program is a little bit like doing a lab project in science—it is a chance to experiment and try new things, while never being quite sure what will happen. For adolescents who prefer active, hands-on activities over sitting and writing, it may become their favorite part of the day. You will be surprised to see the level of excitement and musicality that happens when we allow opportunities for our students to express themselves by creating music spontaneously. And just imagine what the musical world will be like when it is full of musicians who love to improvise!

CHAPTER 4

National Standard 4

National Standard 4: Composing and arranging music within specified guidelines.

(Consortium of National Arts
Education Associations, 1994, 43)

The creative process is a tricky thing. Those who spend much of their lives creating have their own unique approaches, whether the medium is literature, visual arts, or musical composition. Even a quick comparison of Mozart and Haydn will illustrate the point that there is no single creative process, but rather a highly individualized set of strategies for the sometimes exhilarating, sometimes painful phenomenon of making something new. One might wonder if it is really possible to teach someone how to compose; perhaps it might be more realistic to instead work to create opportunities for students to discover their own creativity.

There are several reasons why planning composition activities can be problematic in general music class. For one thing, these activities can be very time-consuming. To create a short melody of even four or eight measures requires time for students to improvise, develop, and revise their musical ideas. Second, writing down the finished melody necessitates at least a rudimentary knowledge of how rhythm, meter, and pitch are notated.

In addition, there are logistical issues in providing instruments for students to use in playing their songs. (Instruments are needed because most general music students cannot look at notation and "hear" the melody.) Whether you use keyboards, resonator bells, recorders, or something else, these materials must be distributed, collected, stored, and maintained. And of course, composition activities can create a high level of chaos in the music room. With careful planning it will be organized chaos, but even that can try the patience of the most saintly teacher by the end of the day!

Finally, assessment of the finished composition can pose another dilemma. How does a teacher (who may or may not count composition as a personal strength) assign a grade to the musical creativity of students?

Many of the above issues can be easily resolved for those who are lucky enough to have a keyboard lab at their disposal. Students can use headphones while working, with the teacher able to listen in through the networked controller. MIDI-compatible keyboards and notation software can be used so that student work is automatically converted to standard notation. There are many fine workshops and classes offered to help teachers design a keyboard lab and learn how to use it. This technology is very motivating to students, but can be cost-prohibitive for some districts.

Those without access to a keyboard lab can still include composition activities in their general music program. One strategy is to plan composition projects that students complete in groups of three or four, using a set of written directions that include a grading rubric. The projects can be designed to enhance the unit currently being studied in class. A unit might include a music theory concept, a brief summary of the life and work of a composer, and a listening lesson. A composition project works well as the culminating activity.

Included in this chapter are three composition projects, along with examples of directions/rubrics for student use and suggested activities that might be used in preparation. As with all the lessons and activities in this book, you may need to make adjustments to better fit your situation and the needs of your students.

If you wish to create a unit of study to accompany a composition project, other lessons might include review of the notation symbols needed for the project and practice in clapping rhythms or playing melodies on piano or resonator bells. It is also helpful to spend time discussing the life and music of a composer who wrote music of the same style or form as the composition to be undertaken.

You will notice that each composition project ends with student performances. Middle school students will likely find it uncomfortable at first to perform for their classmates, and they may become quite concerned about making mistakes. This problem can be solved by being very specific about what is being graded during the performances. The "performance" grade on the sample rubrics (see figures 4.1, 4.2, and 4.3) is determined by the number of hesitations in the final performance, such as stopping or starting over. A count is not kept of wrong notes, as the objective of the activity is to create, notate, and perform a new composition, not necessarily to have a note-perfect performance.

A second strategy to reduce the anxiety of the performers and increase the attentiveness of the audience is represented by the "audience skills" component of the grading rubric. Disruptions during student performances (laughing, making faces, talking, or otherwise distracting the performers) are tallied and included in the final grade.

Another item of note is the inclusion of "teamwork" on the grading rubric. Since the students will complete these projects in a group of three or four, they are expected to work cooperatively. This is not the same thing as taking turns: one student writing a measure while the other three talk or fool around is not good teamwork. All students in the group should be actively engaged at all times. Reminders from the teacher about working as a team reduce the score of the student who needed to be reminded.

The "composition" score on the grading rubric is intended to grade the students' notation of their music, such as their ability to indicate the correct number of beats per measure. There is room on the rubric to award a bonus point for particularly successful compositions, a description that is difficult to quantify, but which is easily recognizable by students and teacher alike.

It should be noted that the rubric score for "composition" is the same for all members of the group, as there will be only one composition per group turned in for grading. However, the scores for "teamwork," "performance," and "audience skills" are individual scores; in this way, students are accountable for their own actions, and are not penalized for the actions of their team members.

When a group activity is introduced, students usually want to know if they will be allowed to choose their own groups. The answer to that question depends largely on the overall behavior and attitude of the whole class. Some classes can easily place themselves in groups, and are likely to work productively most of the time. Other classes are not able to handle this responsibility, and so it will be necessary to assign students to groups based on their achievement level, behavior, and whatever feuds are currently occurring in the class.

Composition Project 1:
The Zipper Bag Project

This is a project that works well at the beginning of the semester, and provides students with an opportunity to expand their comfort zones and personal definitions of music. Be prepared for some unusual sounds!

ACTIVITY 1: IS IT MUSIC?

Materials: Recordings of at least five examples of unusual sounds or music. Try music in another language or from another culture, and music using unusual sound sources. Recordings of sounds from nature (such as whale song) work well.

Time: 5–10 minutes.

Objective: Students will think about their personal definitions of "music" and apply these definition to recorded examples.

Ask students to listen to short recordings (20–30 seconds in length) of unusual sounds or music. At the end of the excerpt, students vote with thumbs up or down to the question, "Is it music?" Usually, by the second or third example, someone will ask what is meant by the word "music." Ask the class to assist in developing a working definition of the word, and then continue with the next recording.

ACTIVITY 2: JOURNAL QUESTION

Materials: Paper and pencil.

Time: 10–15 minutes.

Objective: Students will discover why a standard system of music notation is needed.

Give students about five minutes to write a paragraph that answers the following question: "Why do composers write down their music?" When finished, students may volunteer to read their answers aloud. Possible answers may include the following: "so that they don't forget their music," "so that they can sell their songs," or "so that people can still play their music after their lifetime."

COMPOSITION PROJECT

Materials: Direction/rubric sheet for each student (see figure 4.1 for a sample); paper and pencil; one zipper bag for each group, containing five or six everyday objects that can be used to make sounds. Avoid objects that make very loud sounds and any object that could be used as a weapon or projectile. It is helpful to include a checklist of the objects in each zipper bag for the students to use when cleaning up at the end of the period.

Time: About three 45-minute class periods.

Objective: Students will create sounds with everyday objects, and invent a symbol to represent each sound. Then they will create a composition (30–60 seconds in length) that expresses emotion, and use their symbols to notate it. Each group will perform their composition for the class.

Although the following procedure is written as a single lesson plan, it is likely that it will need to be accomplished over several class periods. It's helpful

Carefully read the rubric that will be used to grade your composition!

1. Using only the materials in the zipper bag, make a list of fifteen sounds that you can create. You may not breathe air on any item to create a sound.
2. Choose the ten sounds you like the most, and create a symbol for each one.
3. Choose an emotion that your composition will express.
4. Using the ten sounds from step 2, create music that expresses the emotion your group chose. Use the symbols you created to write down your music. Your composition must be 30–60 seconds in length.
5. Play through your composition and revise it until all group members are satisfied.
6. Prepare to perform your composition for the class. All group members must participate.

Rubric for Composition 1 **The Zipper Bag Activity**					
	0	1	2	3	4
Teamwork	7 or more reminders, or did not participate	5 or 6 reminders	3 or 4 reminders	1 or 2 reminders	0 reminders
Performance	7 or more hesitations, incomplete, or did not participate	5 or 6 hesitations	3 or 4 hesitations	1 or 2 hesitations	0 hesitations
Audience Skills	7 or more disruptions	5 or 6 disruptions	3 or 4 disruptions	1 or 2 disruptions	0 disruptions
Sounds/Symbols	7 or more missing	5 or 6 missing	3 or 4 missing	1 or 2 missing	Complete: 15 sounds, 10 symbols
Composition	Not enough completed to assess	Very little completed	Up to 10 seconds short **and** incomplete notation	Up to 10 seconds short **or** incomplete notation	Complete: 30–60 seconds, completely notated

Bonus Point (exceptionally successful compositions): ____
Total Points: ____ / 20   Percentage: ____ / 100

Figure 4.1. Directions and Grading Rubric for Composition 1: The Zipper Bag Activity

to collect rubrics and works-in-progress by group, so that redistributing them the next period is less time-consuming.

1. Hand out directions and grading rubrics. Read through each step of the project, and complete a few steps on the chalkboard as an example. Also, read the rubric aloud and explain to students how their work will be graded.
2. Determine a signal that will be used for the teacher to gain the attention of the students (e.g., hand raised, lights turned out) when directions are needed or to announce the time remaining in the class period.
3. Form groups of three or four students, either by assigning students to groups or by allowing students to choose. Distribute the materials.
4. Allow time for students to work with their groups to complete the project as described in the directions. Be sure to circulate among the groups regularly to keep students on task, make note of teamwork reminders that are needed, and provide assistance.
5. When groups finish their work, remind them to practice for their performance.
6. Collect all papers, and ask students to return to their regular seats. Return each group's composition to them when it is their turn to perform, and collect them again when they are finished.

FOLLOW-UP JOURNAL QUESTION

Materials: Paper and pencil.
Time: 10–15 minutes.
Objective: Students will evaluate their compositions using the definition of *music* that the class developed in activity 1.

Give students about five minutes to answer the following question in a paragraph: "Think about the composition that your group created. Is it music? Why or why not?" As in activity 2, encourage students to share their answers with the class.

Composition Project 2: Rhythm Rondo

This project assumes that students understand basic rhythm notation and time signatures, and are able to clap and play rhythms on classroom percussion instruments. The project can be as simple or as complicated as you feel your students can handle—simply change the list of notes/rests that they may use, and lengthen or shorten the number of measures in each section. This project allows students to compose and notate their music without knowledge of treble or bass clefs.

ACTIVITY 1: SAME AND DIFFERENT

Materials: Chalkboard; five signs, one for each letter in rondo form (ABACA). The signs for A, B, and C should be different colors, font styles, and sizes; the three A signs should be the same.
Time: 5–10 minutes.
Objective: Students will discover how composers create contrasting sections in music.

Hold up or post three of the signs, A, B, and C. Ask students to describe how they are different (color, size, font, etc.). Explain that composers often create different sections in their music; just as the signs look different in several ways, sections can sound different in several ways. Ask students to think of ways to make sections sound different, and list key words on the chalkboard (e.g., *fast/slow, loud/soft, staccato/legato, different meters, different instruments*). Explain to students that they will be learning about a particular form of composition called a *rondo*. Hold up or post the signs in the order of a rondo: ABACA.

ACTIVITY 2: RONDO LISTENING LESSON

Materials: Chalkboard, recording of a rondo (two or three minutes in length is ideal), ABACA signs from activity 1.
Time: 10–15 minutes.
Objective: Students will listen to an example of a rondo, recognize the section changes, and describe how the sections are different.

Introduce students to the piece to which they will be listening by writing the title and composer on the chalkboard, and giving any background information that might be helpful. Play the recording of the first A section for the students, and remind them that each time the A section is heard it should sound the same or nearly the same. Play the entire recording, and ask students to raise their hands (or utilize a similar signal) whenever they hear the A section.

Choose five students to come to the front of the room to hold the letter signs. Play the recording again, and have the class give a signal when the next student should hold up his or her sign. Ask students to describe how they recognized section changes (e.g., different tempo, different dynamics, different rhythm).

Carefully read the rubric that will be used to grade your composition!

1. A Section: Write eight measures in $\frac{3}{4}$ time signature, using any notes or rests we've learned so far. Clap your rhythm and revise it until everyone is satisfied.
2. B Section: Write eight measures in $\frac{4}{4}$ time signature. Clap it, and revise as necessary.
3. C Section: Write eight measures in $\frac{3}{5}$ time signature. Clap and revise.
4. Choose a different instrument or combination of instruments for each section. Practice it in rondo form: ABACA. Be sure to make each section sound different by changing the tempo or dynamics.
5. Prepare to perform your composition for the class. All group members must participate.

Rubric for Composition 2 Rhythm Rondo					
	0	1	2	3	4
Teamwork	7 or more reminders, or did not participate	5 or 6 reminders	3 or 4 reminders	1 or 2 reminders	0 reminders
Performance	7 or more hesitations, incomplete, or did not participate	5 or 6 hesitations	3 or 4 hesitations	1 or 2 hesitations	0 hesitations
Audience Skills	7 or more disruptions	5 or 6 disruptions	3 or 4 disruptions	1 or 2 disruptions	0 disruptions
Composition	3 measures completed correctly adds 1 point (24 measures equals 8 points)				
Bonus Point (exceptionally successful compositions): **Total Points:** ___ / 20 Percentage: ___ / 100					

Figure 4.2. Directions and Grading Rubric for Composition 2: Rhythm Rondo

ACTIVITY 3: RECOGNIZING FORM IN A FAMILIAR SONG

Materials: Song sheets/books for a familiar song (choose a song with a verse and a refrain, or an obvious change of section), piano or recorded accompaniment, signs from previous activities.
Time: 5–10 minutes.
Objective: Students will discover the form of a familiar song.

During the course of a regular singing activity, ask students to sing the song you've chosen. After singing it once, ask students how many sections it has. Help students correctly label the sections with A, B, and so on. Choose students to hold up the signs at the appropriate times while the class sings the song again.

COMPOSITION PROJECT

Materials: Direction/rubric sheet for each student (see figure 4.2), paper and pencil, classroom percussion instruments (claves, sandblocks, woodblocks, triangle, sleigh bells, etc.).
Time: About four 45-minute class periods.
Objective: Students will work in groups to create and notate a rhythm composition in rondo form, using contrasting time signatures. Students will perform their completed compositions for the class.

This composition project can be introduced using the same procedure as in the first project. You may wish to provide paper for each group with time signatures and bar lines already printed, so that students can begin composing right away. When students are ready to prepare their performances, consider having groups take turns practicing with the instruments, in order to keep the volume level in the classroom at a manageable level.

Composition Project 3: Theme and Variations

In this project, students will use a melody that they already know well, and create three variations. One possibility to use for this project is "Ode to Joy." It may be easier to use only the first two phrases, transposed to the key of C. However, another eight-measure melody can be easily substituted; be advised that a longer melody will mean that more time is required for students to complete their compositions. It is helpful to choose a melody that students can already sing and play on bells or piano; they will be more successful in creating variations when they know the theme very well. Knowledge of basic rhythm notation, meter signatures, and treble-clef notes is needed.

ACTIVITY 1: CREATING VARIATIONS TO A FAMILIAR SONG

Materials: Song sheets/books for a familiar song, piano accompaniment, chalkboard.

Time: 10–15 minutes.

Objective: Students will sing a familiar song several times, varying the tempo, dynamics, rhythm, and/or texture.

During a regular singing activity, ask students to sing a familiar song. After singing it once, ask students to try singing it at a very different tempo. Then try changing the dynamics, the number of students singing, or part of the rhythm. Help the class choose the three most successful *variations* (begin using the term at this time), and write on the chalkboard the order in which they will perform them, beginning with the *theme* (i.e., the familiar version). Perform the theme and variations in the order determined by the class. Explain to students that they will be learning about a form of composition called *theme and variations*, in which the composer makes changes to a melody.

ACTIVITY 2: THEME AND VARIATIONS LISTENING LESSON

Materials: Paper and pencil, recording of an example of theme and variations (such as Mozart's *Ah vous dirai-je, Maman* or Copland's variations on "Simple Gifts").

Time: 15 minutes.

Objective: Students will listen to an example of theme and variations, and discover how the composer made changes in each variation.

Ask students to write down the title and composer of the piece they will listen to, and provide any background information that may be helpful. Listen to the theme, and help students discover the song. (It's fun to make this a surprise.) Then listen to at least three variations, one at a time. While listening, ask students to jot down what they hear that is different from the theme; allow for time after each variation, or at the end, for students to share their thoughts.

ACTIVITY 3: THEME AND VARIATIONS IN VISUAL ART

Materials: Paper; pencil; crayons; colored pencils; markers; prints or computer images of at least three pieces of visual art by the same artist that explore the same theme (Monet's haystack paintings, George Rodrigue's blue-dog paintings, or something similar).

Time: 20–30 minutes.

Objective: Students will discover how visual artists use theme and variations to produce artwork. They will also create a theme and variations drawing.

Using the prints or projected computer images, show students several pieces of art by the same artist that explore a theme. Ask students to find ways that the variations are the same and different from one another.

Distribute a sheet of drawing paper to each student, and ask them to fold the paper into quarters. Then allow students to use pencils, colored pencils, crayons, or markers to create four drawings that depict the same object, using different sizes, colors, textures, and so on. If time allows, give students a chance to show their drawings to the class. Remind students that just as visual artists can vary color, size, and texture, composers can vary tempo, dynamics, texture, and timbre. The completed drawings will make a very nice bulletin board display.

COMPOSITION PROJECT

Materials: Direction/rubric sheet for each student (see figure 4.3); staff paper and pencil; melody instrument for each group, such as resonator bells, keyboards, or recorders.

Time: About four 45-minute class periods.

Objective: Students will create three variations of a familiar melody by changing the rhythm, melody, and form of the theme. They will perform their theme and variations for the class.

Introduce the project using the same procedure as for composition 1. You may want to consider providing staff paper for each group that has the theme already written, and the bar lines set up for each variation.

Admittedly, composing "by committee" is not how all musicians prefer to create new material. However, there are several advantages to group compositions in middle school general music. Adolescents are naturally very social, and this provides an opportunity for collaboration. In addition, for those teachers who must work with large classes, there are fewer compositions to guide and assess. It also provides a nice change of pace from whole-group instruction for both teacher and students.

Some young musicians may find that composition is not for them; after all, the same thing is also true for adult musicians. But for others, you just might be lighting a spark that could ignite a bonfire of creativity. Those are the kids who will start keeping a notebook full of lyrics, or who will begin playing their own ideas on the keyboard. Fan the flames by allowing volunteers to share their musical ideas with the class at the end of a period, or by permitting them to visit the music room before school for extra composition time. You just might discover the next shining light of creative genius.

Carefully read the rubric that will be used to grade your composition!

1. Use the melody instrument to play through your theme.
2. Create the first variation by changing the rhythm of the theme. You must change at least one thing in each measure. You may do this in several ways:
   - Change a quarter note to two eighth notes on the same line or space.
   - Change a quarter note to a quarter rest. That beat will now be silent.
   - Change two eighth notes that are on the same line or space to one quarter note.
3. Create the second variation by changing the melody of the first variation. You may change any line/space to any other line/space in the C scale. You must change at least one note in each measure.
4. Create the third variation by changing the second variation in one of the following ways:
   - Change the form by writing the measures in a different order.
   - Dramatically change the tempo or dynamics several times throughout the piece.
5. Play your composition and revise it until everyone in your group is satisfied.
6. Choose four people from your group to perform your composition for the class, one for the theme and one for each variation. The other group members should help them prepare and practice. Someone from the group can help by pointing to the notes during the performance.

Rubric for Composition 3 Theme and Variations					
	0	1	2	3	4
Teamwork	7 or more reminders, or did not participate	5 or 6 reminders	3 or 4 reminders	1 or 2 reminders	0 reminders
Performance	7 or more hesitations, incomplete, or did not participate	5 or 6 hesitations	3 or 4 hesitations	1 or 2 hesitations	0 hesitations
Audience Skills	7 or more disruptions	5 or 6 disruptions	3 or 4 disruptions	1 or 2 disruptions	0 disruptions
Composition	Each variation is worth 3 points (9 points total)				

Bonus Point (exceptionally successful compositions):
Total Points: ___ / 20   Percentage: ___ / 100

Figure 4.3.   Directions and Grading Rubric for Composition 3: Theme and Variations

CHAPTER 5

National Standard 5

National Standard 5: Reading and notating music.

(Consortium of National Arts
Education Associations, 1994, 44)

Imagine for a moment that you are required to learn a new language. This new language uses a different alphabet. And every one of these new symbols means two things simultaneously. Oh, and by the way, no one in your family can read this new language. One more thing—you only get to go to class once or twice a week. Are you ready for the test yet?

Okay, now let's call this new language . . . hmm . . . how about *music*?

Actually, that's how many of our students feel. I must admit, I sometimes forget that not everyone learns to read music notation the same way that I did—as a young child, raised in a musical family, where practicing an instrument was part of the daily routine. Learning to read music at the same time as learning to read words is an ideal way to learn such a complicated symbol system.

However, learning to read music is a bit more of a challenge for many adolescents. For one thing, some students speak a different language at home than they do at school; music is essentially their third language. Also, due to the mobile lifestyle of contemporary society, not all have enjoyed the benefit of a solid, consistent musical foundation in elementary school. Third, making music is not part of daily life for every student, the way it was for me at their age.

Sometimes I catch myself saying things that make perfect sense to me, but which are completely illogical to my students. For example, can we really call a quarter note "the black note" when it is drawn with yellow chalk on a green chalkboard? And who decided that the "first" line of the staff should be on the bottom, when in every other class the first line is at the top of the page? Not to mention the fact that only in music class would we draw a symbol upside down and treat it as the same thing—just try doing that in math class with the number 6!

Good teaching (of anything) begins with what the students already know and ends with what we want them to know. Once we understand these first two variables, we can plan activities that systematically take them from one to the other. So let's begin by considering three questions: What prior knowledge do our students have about music notation? What should our students know and be able to do at the end of this course? What methods will we use to teach our objectives?

What prior knowledge do our students have about music notation?
• What have our students been taught in previous years, and do they remember any of it?
• Do all of the students have about the same level of knowledge, or are there some students who play instruments or have taken private lessons?

What should our students know and be able to do at the end of this course?
• Which rhythm notes are we planning to teach? Dotted rhythms? Syncopation?
• How much time do we want to spend on meter concepts? Should we teach $\frac{6}{8}$ and cut time, or only the time signatures with a 4 on the bottom?
• Should we cover treble clef, bass clef, or both?
• Would we like students to understand terms like *forte* and *allegro*, or should we only use English equivalents?
• How about key signatures, major/minor tonality, and chord symbols?
• Is it enough for students to understand the basic idea, or are we aiming for students who can read music as easily as they read words?
• Does the school, district, or state have a music curriculum that makes these decisions for us?

What methods will we use to teach our objectives?
• Will music-theory instruction be part of every lesson?
• Should we teach mnemonic devices ("Every Good Boy," etc.), or is that just a crutch?
• Should we use a fixed *do*, a movable *do*, or letter names?
• Should we do sight singing? Dictation?
• Will we say, *ta ta titi ta*, or "One and two and . . ."?
• Will we employ Orff, Kodaly, or another specific methodology? Or is an eclectic approach more appropriate?

As much as I might like to interject my own opinions here, I cannot answer these questions for you. You know your students, and you know what is appropriate for them; no knowledgeable college professor, influential state-curriculum chair, or well-meaning author enjoys the daily interactions with your students that you do. Before you continue reading, you may wish to go back and think about the above questions, and how their answers are embedded in the music education you are providing for your students.

The rest of this chapter contains strategies for teaching and reinforcing music-notation skills. Each of these ideas can and should be modified to fit your situation. Concepts can be simplified or made more complex, depending on the age of your students, the amount of time you have with them, and the objectives you are working to address.

Many of these activities are games, so let's take a moment to think about prizes. It's not always wise to award prizes to a few students, leaving the rest to frustration and resentment. This can create a substantial disruption; although it may seem silly to adults to fight about a lollipop or sticker, it is not unusual for middle school students to do just that. In my room, the prize for any game is always the same: "The Love and Joy of Learning." When students complain, I remind them about just how boring I can be when I put my mind to it, so they might as well enjoy the game while it lasts.

Rhythm-Card Activities

Although I now teach in a music room with many instruments and supplies, I have not always been so lucky. There's nothing that will test your creativity faster than trying to occupy middle school students in a room that contains only student and teacher desks! These activities require only minimal supplies—a stack of large index cards and a marker. On each card, draw a rhythm note and write its name underneath. Make several cards for each note that you are teaching, and be sure to include rests. You might also make a card for rhythm patterns such as syncopation, and dotted quarter/eighth. Keep these cards in an envelope and store them someplace where you can find them easily, like on top of the piano or on your cart.

There are lots of things you can do with a set of rhythm cards. These activities are especially helpful because they can be stretched or condensed to fit the time frame available—they can fill up five extra minutes at the end of the period, or fifteen minutes at the beginning of a lesson.

CREATE AND CLAP RHYTHMS

Choose four students to come to the front of the room, and hand each a note or rest that has a value of one beat. As the volunteers hold up their cards, the remainder of the class claps the rhythm. Sounds easy, right? There are many variations to this activity, and they can be surprisingly challenging:

- When the first rhythm is successfully clapped, ask the volunteers to place themselves in a different order; then clap the new rhythm.
- Choose another student to determine the order of the cards.
- Replace cards, so that each beat is a different note or rest.
- Add four more volunteers and cards, and ask the class to clap two measures instead of one.
- If the class is having trouble clapping a rhythm accurately, challenge volunteers to clap it alone. When one student has succeeded, gradually add a few more students at a time until everyone has clapped the rhythm correctly.
- Clap the rhythm for the class, intentionally making an error on one beat. Ask the class to find your mistake.
- Clap the rhythm backward.
- Divide the class into two groups. Group A claps the rhythm forward while Group B claps the rhythm backward—at the same time.
- Have group A clap the first measure at the same time that group B claps the second measure.
- Clap the rhythm as a two- or three-part canon.
- Are your volunteers getting too wiggly? Ask them to hand their cards to friends, and then sit down to join the rest of the class.
- Replace a quarter-note card with a half-note card. Help the class discover that the rhythm now has too many beats, and choose another card to remove. Ask two students to hold the half-note card, visually reinforcing that this note gets two beats.
- Do the same with a dotted half note, a whole note, or a pattern that is worth more than one beat, such as dotted quarter and eighth note.

Of course, it's best to not try all of these ideas on the same day. Middle school students tend to do very well for about ten or fifteen minutes, and then it's time to move on to something else.

DICTATION

Although you may have less than happy memories of dictation from your college days, it is possible to include activities in which students are challenged to hear a rhythm and discover how to notate it. As long as the notes are visually represented in some way, the students don't necessarily have to be doing the writing themselves.

Step 1: Line up all your rhythm cards on the chalk tray at the front of the room. Review with students what each note sounds like, and how many beats it is worth.

Step 2: Clap a rhythm, and have students echo it. Start simply, with a four-beat rhythm that includes only two different notes. Subsequent examples can be longer and more complex.

Step 3: Randomly choose a student to come to the front of the room and pick the card that represents the first beat of the rhythm. To reduce the pressure, tell students that they can ask for the rhythm to be repeated as often as they like, and they can ask someone in the class to help them. When the correct note card has been chosen, the student stands at the front of the room with the card.

Step 4: Continue choosing students to select a card, one beat at a time, until the entire rhythm has been "notated."

Step 5: Clap the rhythm again, and ask the class if the note cards are correct.

This activity can be varied in several ways. Try having students write a rhythm of four or eight beats on scrap paper. Collect all the rhythms, and choose one at random for the class to "notate." Also, once a rhythm has been correctly "notated," write it on the chalkboard. After several rhythms have been recorded, clap them in canon, or use them as ostinati during a song or instrumental activity.

FLASH CARDS

This probably seems obvious, but your rhythm cards make good flash cards. Cover up the name of the note with your hand, and ask students to identify it. Quiz students on the beat values in different time signatures. Better yet, choose a student to be in charge of flash-card review while you take attendance.

While we're on the subject, this may be a good time to mention ways to make flash cards more engaging for our students. These ideas will work for bass clef, treble clef, key signatures, or anything else that requires drill and practice.

- Be sure everyone in the class can see the card before calling on a student to answer; it's only fair, and allows for a little bit of "thinking time."
- When a student answers correctly, hand the next card to him or her, and allow this student to choose the next person. If it seems that students are calling only on their best friends, require them to alternate boys and girls.
- Plan a "speed round" to see how many correct answers can be achieved within sixty seconds.

- If you want to motivate the more competitive students, post a "high score" board in your room; the video gamers in the class will perk right up!
- Remember, when it comes to flash cards, a little goes a very long way. Three or four minutes of drill are plenty; more than five minutes is a guaranteed way to lose your students' interest.

Rhythm Tic-Tac-Toe

A number of years ago at a state Music Education Association conference, this gem was presented by Gary Travis, music teacher at the Masterman School in Philadelphia. The only supplies you will need are paper and pencil for each student.

On Your Mark: To create a game board, each student draws a large tic-tac-toe grid on a piece of paper. In every box, students are to notate a four-beat rhythm, using only quarter notes, eighth notes (in pairs), and quarter rests. It is not required that each rhythm include each type of note.

Get Set: It is important that students know what their rhythms sound like, so think of as many ways as possible to get them clapping. Provide a strong "ready, go," and ask all students to clap their middle boxes at the same time—yes, it will sound a little crazy, but middle schoolers thrive on chaos anyway. Move on to the whole top row; then a box where every note is the same; perhaps the four corner boxes; next, a rhythm with a quarter rest on beat 3; their favorite rhythm; and anything else you can come up with. Now they're familiar with the rhythms they've created, and you have kept them busy while the last few stragglers finished setting up their game boards.

Go: Using a list of four-beat rhythms that you've prepared ahead of time, clap a rhythm for the students and ask them to echo it. Then have students look on their game boards to find that rhythm. If it is there, they can draw an X on it (or a star, a happy face, their initials, or whatever they choose). You may need to clap the rhythm several times and, if you wish, call on a volunteer to tell classmates which notes were clapped. The first student to get three boxes in a row is the winner, but don't stop there—keep going until time or your students' interest runs out.

It's All in Your Head

I stumbled on this particular strategy by accident while trying to fill up a few extra minutes at the end of a period. It is particularly helpful for the aural learners in your class. It could be used to review other things, but this example will use rhythm skills. Here is an example of how it might be introduced:

> Okay, when I count you in, I want you to clap four quarter notes. One, two, ready, go.
> Now, this time, please clap two eighth notes on the third beat. Ready, go.
> That was nicely done. Let's try moving the eighth notes to the second beat instead.
> Leave the eighth notes on beat 2, and add a quarter rest on beat 4.
> Let's clap that rhythm again, and add a whole note after it.
> Change the whole note to two half notes, but leave the first four beats the same.

It doesn't take long before good-natured confusion reigns, but it's amazing how quickly the students will rise to the challenge.

Relay "Races"

These activities work well to review information that requires memorization. They can be easily included in lessons shortly before a test, as a good way to determine if students are prepared. Be sure you have enough time to complete the entire activity—the last step is probably the most important, so don't try to squeeze this one into the last few minutes of the period. You will need a stack of 3″ × 5″ index cards, preferably in different colors (or use different colored markers), long envelopes, and a place to hang them. A stopwatch or a clock with a second hand is also necessary.

TREBLE-CLEF RELAY

Create four sets of cards, using a different colored card for each set (or use a different colored marker for each set). On each card, draw a staff and a treble clef sign, and then draw a whole note on one of the lines or spaces you have taught. You will also need seven long envelopes. Label each with a letter, A through G, and post them at the front of the room so that cards can be placed inside.

Divide your class into four teams. Teams complete the relay one at a time; they do not race each other (a disaster waiting to happen), but rather "race" against the clock. The winning team is determined by the number of correct answers within the specified time.

First: Team 1 stands in a line. Hand a card to the first student in line; he or she determines the letter name of the note, places it in the (hopefully) correct envelope, and then goes to the back of the line. (Be sure to think about traffic flow for this activity.) When the first student has finished, hand a card to the next student in line. Continue until all cards have been placed in envelopes, or until ninety seconds have passed, whichever comes first. Each student is expected to work alone, as there is not enough time allotted for a consultation with team members.

Next: Repeat this process with each of the other teams.

Finally: It's time to tally the scores. Draw a point chart on the chalkboard with a column for each team (each team's name is the color of its cards), and ask a student to make tally marks at your direction.

Remove all the cards from the first envelope. Ask students to describe to you what the correct answer(s) should look like—first line, second space, and so forth. Then have students help you determine which cards are correct, and award one point for each correct answer. Continue until all the cards have been scored. The team with the most points receives your congratulations and bragging rights.

Here's the really sneaky part—only the individual students know if their cards were placed in the correct envelope. Their understanding of treble-clef notes has been tested without the usual fear of failure or ridicule. Remind students that if they were unsure of how to figure out the name of a note, they should review before the test. Be sure to point out common mistakes as they become apparent, such as mixing up middle C and the D right above it.

BASS-CLEF RELAY

Complete this relay in the same manner as the treble-clef relay, but make sets of bass-clef cards. For a real challenge, combine treble-clef and bass-clef sets, and allow three minutes for each team.

DYNAMIC-MARKS RELAY

Each set of cards includes a card with an Italian term (e.g., fortissimo) and another card with the abbreviation (*ff*). The envelopes are labeled with the English translations ("very loud"). The rest of the game is played as above.

Name That Tune

The really challenging part of reading music notation is to put together all of the skills that have been taught separately: clapping rhythms, reading lines and spaces, understanding key and time signatures, and following directions such as repeat signs, D.S. al coda, and so on. This activity provides an opportunity for students to work together to accomplish this goal.

On staff paper, write the notation for several short songs that your students will recognize, such as "Happy Birthday," "Frère Jacques," and so forth. Divide students into groups of three or four, and provide instruments for them to use. (Choose instruments you use in class, and be sure that you have at least one for each group. Keyboards, resonator bells, and recorders all work.) For your own sanity, set clear expectations about safe use of the instruments, appropriate sound level, and the signal you will use to gain their attention.

Challenge your students to play the songs from notation and identify the titles. For added interest, include four or five songs on each sheet, in order of difficulty. If your students enjoy games, assign point values for playing and identifying each song, with a time limit for the activity.

Poetry in Motion

Choose a poem that is relatively short (eight to twelve lines), and challenge students to work in small groups to prepare a dramatic reading of it. Each line should be marked with a dynamic level or a tempo marking—only proper terminology, please! Give each group an opportunity to present the poem to the class. My favorite poems to use are "A Minor Bird" by Robert Frost and "How Not to Have to Dry the Dishes" by Shel Silverstein. (Yes, you will have to tell them what drying the dishes means.)

Make Notation Part of Every Activity

The more our students use notation, the more adept they will become. So now it's time to do what teachers do best—find ways for our students to learn without even realizing it. Try a few of these ideas to infuse notation into every part of your lesson:

• Ask students to identify the time and/or key signatures whenever a new song is introduced in class.

- Teach instrumental parts from notation. When students are focused on playing the instrument correctly, they don't notice how much notation they're reviewing.
- Whenever possible, put notation in front of students while they're singing. Try to avoid using song sheets that contain lyrics only.
- Post the notation of the important theme or motive as part of a listening lesson.
- Use notation as a reference point: "Let's start from the half note in the second measure."
- Use proper terms, and slide in a quick explanation: "Let's try the A section at a forte level to see if we like singing the beginning loudly."
- During an improvisation activity, challenge students to notate one or two of the most successful improvised passages. Post them on a "hall of fame" display.
- Use bulletin boards to teach and reinforce notation skills. Try a "song of the month" board that includes notation, along with student artwork inspired by it.

Our long-term goal for teaching music notation should be to make ourselves obsolete—if we do our jobs well, our students won't need us anymore. I'd like to think that one day in the future my students will have the occasion to look at a piece of sheet music. They will certainly not remember everything I taught them, and they may not even remember my name. But I hope they have a few ideas about how to decipher the notes on the page, and can perhaps pick out a few phrases on the piano. At the very least, they will know that music is a discipline with specific knowledge and skills that can be learned by anyone with the motivation to do so, including themselves.

CHAPTER 6

National Standard 6

National Standard 6: Listening to, analyzing, and describing music.

(Consortium of National Arts
Education Associations, 1994, 44)

Note: This chapter was previously published as "Meaningful Listening for Middle and High School Students" (McAnally 2007).

The first time I asked my middle school music students to listen to Beethoven's Fifth Symphony, I was very nervous. We had been studying the composer's life, and I wanted them to feel a connection to his music. I was afraid that they wouldn't take it seriously. Very quickly, these students surprised me with their willingness to listen to something new. Beethoven was just the tip of the iceberg: I soon realized that with careful planning, my students would listen to all kinds of things. Now, listening activities are a regular part of my program.

Listening is an important skill for all of us, but it's critical for musicians and those who love music. National Standard 6 calls for students to listen to, analyze, and describe a wide variety of music. This listening, analysis, and description can pose challenges for older students who are familiar with a narrow repertoire and accustomed to music as background to other activities. In addition, many middle and high school students have already developed strong musical preferences that are an integral part of their sense of identity. Planning activities that create meaningful connections between students and diverse listening selections can be an overwhelming proposition. However, with careful planning, listening can become an exciting component of secondary music programs.

45

Objectives for Listening

The first step in planning a meaningful listening experience is to think carefully about the objectives. Listening lessons are often planned to reinforce concepts or topics taught at another time. For example, when you're teaching about unusual time signatures, Dave Brubeck's "Unsquare Dance" might be a logical choice to convey the concept, and a recording of Louis Armstrong's "Heebie Jeebies" is a good way to illustrate scat singing. Just as literacy teachers teach vocabulary in context rather than in isolation, music concepts and vocabulary must be placed in musical context for students to construct meaning from them.

Other, broader objectives are also important. Carefully chosen selections tied to well-designed, open-ended questions can encourage students to think like musicians as they consider the effects of composers' choices on the listener. Listening to music from diverse time periods, cultures, and styles will help students expand their personal definitions of the word *music*, opening new horizons and creating what will, we hope, become a lifelong relationship with music. Introducing students to pieces that express a wide range of emotional content can help them acknowledge these emotions as part of the human experience and help them find in music a safe haven for their self-expression.

Choosing Repertoire

Choosing material with which students can build a connection is very important. Of course, we would like students to be willing and able to listen to anything, but teachers know that some pieces are more likely to provide a successful experience than others.

The length of the selection is an important consideration. If multiple listenings are planned, choose a shorter piece. If a longer piece is chosen, plan on spending a longer amount of time preparing students for the listening experience. Keep in mind that what may seem like a short work to us as music professionals can seem like an eternity to middle or high school students. You will likely find that two to three minutes is a comfortable length, and anything over five minutes requires very careful preparation. If you wish to choose a larger work, consider playing representative portions rather than the whole piece.

Try to choose music that has something to draw the listener in. Quotations from familiar songs or catchy themes are helpful. A fast tempo and a strong rhythmic feel can tap into students' natural exuberance, and a "surprise" partway through is also fun. Be careful not to limit the selections to traditional orchestral fare or pieces that personally appeal to you; middle and high school students may surprise you with a delight in dissonance, atonality, and nontraditional sound sources.

Another consideration is whether the piece has lyrics. Words open another dimension to musical communication. However, students sometimes focus on the lyrics, missing other important aspects of a piece. In addition, they may be distracted by the differences in vocal style between the teacher's selection and what is currently popular. If you wish to choose a vocal piece, choose carefully, and prepare students for what they will hear and how they will be expected to respond.

Teachers must consider educational soundness along with listener appeal when selecting music for students. Ideally, listening lessons should support the objectives and concepts being covered in class. You may also wish to include pieces that are representative of a particular genre or style, as well as pieces with such inherent value that they are considered necessary to musical literacy. It's absolutely crucial that listening lessons represent the widest range of musical expression: diverse genres, styles, periods, and cultures must be included. Avoid referring to music as "yours" or "mine"—all music has something to say to all of us.

Occasionally, it may be helpful to allow your students to choose music for listening experiences and perhaps even lead the lesson. Have a frank discussion with the class ahead of time about what is appropriate for school with regard to lyrics, and don't be afraid to require that students present their choices to you beforehand. You always have the right to veto any selection. Be fair, allow all students an equal opportunity for this privilege, and require the class to listen with respect to the choices of their peers. Middle and high school students are highly invested in their musical preferences and will not hesitate to defend them vehemently; careful preparation is required to avoid conflicts.

Finding Student-Friendly Listening Examples

- Ask students about their favorite radio stations. Tune in to one of these during your morning commute to get a sense of students' extracurricular listening.
- Keep a list handy to jot down song titles and artists. This information can become the basis for interesting future lessons. You never know when you'll hear something new and relevant.
- Consider investing in an MP3 player. Song files can be downloaded for a small fee and stored easily. This prevents you from having to buy an entire CD for only a single track. You can also create a playlist with all the listening selections in order for a particular lesson.

Preparation for Listening

Once appropriate selections are chosen, it's time to plan for a positive listening lesson. Effective listening experiences have three parts: preparation, listening, and follow-up. Depending on the length and objectives of the particular lesson, the first and last components may be very short; but for the purpose of this discussion, assume that a longer activity is planned.

In the preparation phase, the goal is to build bridges between the students and the music. Since students come to the classroom with different perspectives, experiences, and backgrounds, more than one bridge must be constructed, not unlike the variety of approaches used to accommodate multiple learning styles.

One way to begin is to explore the life of the composer. Look for an event or personality trait with which your students might identify, and tell it like a story. Tell students about how Beethoven was able to continue to compose after becoming deaf as an adult. Let them know that Bach had twenty children by two wives and that several sons became composers as well. Fill them in about Louis Armstrong's youthful run-ins with the law, which led to his musical beginnings.

Use other resources to paint as complete a picture as possible of the composer's experiences. Read the first chapter of John Steinbeck's *The Grapes of Wrath* and newspaper accounts of the Dust Bowl years in the American West to present the environment that inspired many Woody Guthrie songs. Help students understand that composers are real people who have triumphs and tragedies like everyone else.

Once students feel a connection with the composer, prepare them for what they will hear. If the piece includes themes derived from other songs, sing them together. Notate short themes or motives on the board, and have students play or sing them. Display pictures of the instruments that are included, provide translations of non-English lyrics, or teach the conducting pattern for the meter of the selection.

Listening

Now students are ready to listen to the music. But how can we be sure that they're actively listening and not just staring into space? The answer is to find a "hook" that will grab and keep their attention; that hook is different for each piece.

One solution to this problem is to use a listening map. These graphic representations of the music are often available through basal music series; they can also be created by teachers or students. By focusing the students' eyes, listening maps can help focus their attention as well. A word of caution, however: Don't overuse visual cues. Leave room for students to interact with music internally on their own terms.

Another way is to encourage students to raise a hand or give a silent signal when something specific is heard. For example, students can signal whenever they hear the familiar song "Clementine" while listening to the Charles Ives piece "The Gong on the Hook and Ladder." The list of target sounds should be just long enough to keep students focused, but not so long that they cannot enjoy what they are hearing.

If the listening selection includes a short motive, try asking students to keep a tally of the number of times the motive is heard. Luvenia George has written a detailed lesson plan (available online) using this strategy for Duke Ellington's piece "Koko," in which the composer conjures the Congo Square drum ceremonies in New Orleans (George, 1999a, 1999b). This approach is appropriate for other pieces as well, such as the first movement of Beethoven's Symphony no. 5. Advise students in advance that because individual listeners hear different things in the same piece of music, the class will probably arrive at a range of answers. Although it's fun to compare, the point of the activity is not simply to discover one "correct" answer. Rather, the goal is to discover how a composer can use repetition and variation to create a work of art from one short idea.

Some pieces of music lend themselves to playing or singing along. For example, students can easily play chord tones on mallet instruments or piano as they listen to a recording of Pachelbel's Canon in D.

Journal writing during and after listening is also very effective. Give students an open-ended question to consider as they listen, and allow time for them to jot down their thoughts. For example: What do you hear? What emotions do you think the composer is trying to express? Do you hear any changes during the piece? What kind of story do you think the composer is trying to tell? Many students find it easier to respond with shapes, colors, and images rather than words. Gather some materials, and give students free rein to express themselves in a manner inspired by the listening selection. Students may be willing to display their writing and artwork on a bulletin board, but be sensitive to students' need for privacy, and ask permission first.

As students are working on their responses to the listening activity you've chosen, do the same thing yourself. Find a place to sit, get out paper and pencil, and answer journal questions or count motives along with the students. You may be surprised what new things you will hear each time, and students will learn from your example that careful listening is a rewarding activity for adults as well as students.

Follow-Up

The follow-up portion of the lesson is very important as students make sense of their listening. Give students a chance to share their answers, and share yours as well. Remind students many times and in many ways that there is more than one right answer—composers want listeners to make personal and unique connections with the work. To encourage thoughtful answers, ask specific questions about students' responses, such as "Did the tempo and dynamics of this piece influence your answer?" As you moderate the discussion, be clear that you are looking for carefully considered ideas, not judgments.

It's important to allow for appropriate expression of opinions at the close of the lesson. Insist on answers that are respectful of the composer's work of art, but allow students to express negative viewpoints. You might consider a three-point rating system:

- 1 = "I like it so much that I might consider listening to it on my own time or purchasing a recording of it."
- 2 = "I liked it somewhat, but would probably not choose this music for myself."
- 3 = "This is really not my favorite music, but I respect the composer for expressing his or her ideas."

Middle and high school students have clear musical preferences, and a teacher who shows respect for this gains a great deal of credibility. Praise students for listening with an open mind and being willing to try something unfamiliar.

Tips for Better Listening in the Classroom
- Consider beginning each class with a brief listening activity. Students will come to expect this and look forward to it. They can't master listening if they don't practice it.
- Use a variety of media for student responses. Some students enjoy writing, whereas others would rather convey their ideas through the visual arts. Give listeners a chance to try several forms of expression.
- Involve students in the choice of listening material. Every student should have a chance to share a favorite piece (approved by you) and should come prepared to present a short biography or description of the work of the composer or performer.
- Try listening to several versions of the same piece. For example, many artists have recorded standards like "Sweet Georgia Brown" and "Pennies from Heaven." It can be interesting to compare two or three recordings.

- Don't be discouraged if students are initially resistant to listening activities. They may not be accustomed to careful, objective listening. Teach students the desired attitude, and provide lots of positive feedback.
- Some listening activities can be planned as games. Challenge students to listen to short excerpts and correctly identify the country of origin, the composer, the style, or the title. Students can work in teams to get the most correct answers.

Many of the other National Standards are included in the listening activities that have been described here. As students prepare to listen, they will likely be reading notation as they sing or play themes (Standards 1, 2, and 5). Students will also explore the historical and cultural context in which the piece was created as they learn about the composer (Standards 8 and 9). The listening portion of the lesson allows students to listen, analyze, and describe (Standard 6), and sometimes play or sing along (Standards 1 and 2). The follow-up activities often include an opportunity to evaluate what has been heard (Standard 7).

Clearly, listening experiences are important in creating well-rounded musicians. When we choose material carefully, prepare our students fully, and present activities that encourage active listening, we build meaningful connections between our students and music. By challenging ourselves and our students to listen to, analyze, and describe a diverse selection of music, we open up a whole new world of musical possibilities.

CHAPTER 7

National Standard 7

National Standard 7: Evaluating music and music performances.

(Consortium of National Arts
Education Associations, 1994, 44)

If there's one thing a middle school student has plenty of, it's opinions! If your students are anything like mine, they will have no problem telling you what they think of just about anything, from the temperature in your classroom, to your new haircut, to the real-world (ir)relevance of your lesson plans.

However strongly held and vehemently stated they may be, these opinions are often based on a fairly narrow set of poorly articulated criteria. When students are asked why they like a particular song, the most likely answer in my room is, "I like the beat." When asked why a song is not to their liking, the response will probably be, "It's corny." Clearly, forming an opinion is not the problem. Being able to state an opinion appropriately and support it with objective reasoning are the necessary next steps.

In all honesty, this is a tough standard to teach. No matter how objective one might try to be, evaluating musical performances is an inherently subjective enterprise. Perhaps this is why we sometimes avoid the topic altogether. We might say to ourselves, "Who are we to make a judgment about someone else's self expression?" Or perhaps we are afraid to make our students more opinionated than they already are.

Regardless of the reasons for our hesitancy, learning to make and support evaluations is an important life skill. Students who learn to judge without being judgmental, and to self-evaluate without losing self-esteem, will be more successful in both the adult and the musical worlds.

In this chapter we will consider two ways to incorporate evaluation into our general music programs. The first method is to enhance existing lessons with short activities that encourage students to make musical evaluations based on objective criteria. The second idea takes the form of a music critics unit, in which students will write a critique using a recording of their own choice.

Approach 1: Evaluation as a Daily Activity

Our first approach to teaching students how to evaluate musical performances is to make it a part of the daily routine. Giving students frequent opportunities to voice their opinions within clearly defined parameters provides practice at this skill. It is also very motivating for students to feel that their thoughts matter.

The strategy is simple: Look at your existing lesson plan on any topic, and add a short activity in which students are asked to make an evaluation based on the concept just taught. The activity can be as straightforward as answering a question or two, orally or in writing, or it might be a bit more complex. Either way, it should be a short enhancement of the lesson, not a lengthy addition to it.

A focus on appropriate use of music vocabulary is relevant here. When students answer an evaluation question, you might rephrase their answers for the class using proper terminology. Or ask follow-up questions until students are able to include the correct words in their answers.

There are many opportunities for minilessons in evaluation that can be incorporated into other activities. Even a small addition to your plan can help students learn to make musical evaluations based on clearly defined criteria, while simultaneously supporting the original objective of the lesson. Here are a few ideas to try:

- After a lesson on diction, choose one or two students to listen to the class sing and make a list of all the words that were not pronounced clearly. Sing the song again to see if the class can improve their diction.
- Have the class sing the same song twice, and then evaluate which performance was better. Be sure to ask students to explain their opinions using music vocabulary.
- Ask students to perform a song on the piano at two different tempos, and decide which tempo is more effective. If the class can't remember what *andante* and *allegro* mean, show them where they can look up the information.
- Listen to recordings of the same song performed by two different artists, and discuss with the class which performance was most successful and why. If you

wish to expand this activity, use a Venn diagram to help students organize their thoughts. This strategy works well when studying jazz, in order to highlight the unique strengths of each artist.

- After a small group performs an original composition (see chapter 5), ask the student audience what they liked best about it. Ask clarifying questions to encourage answers that are specific and detailed.
- When engaging students in a listening activity, ask them to consider what the composer was trying to accomplish (e.g., tell a story, create a mood). When the class achieves consensus in their answer, ask if they feel the composer was successful in accomplishing that goal.
- Have students look at a short example of music notation while you sing or play it. Insert two or three wrong notes, and challenge students to find your mistakes.
- When grading student work using a rubric, allow students to evaluate themselves before viewing your evaluation. Or, if time allows, complete your evaluation together during a short student/teacher conference.

When evaluation activities are interwoven into daily lessons, students are regularly encouraged to form an opinion and support it with musical reasons. They will become less likely to form snap judgments and more likely to be objective and open-minded. In addition, when concepts are applied to an evaluation, the students' understanding of these concepts is further reinforced.

Approach 2: Music Critics Unit

Another approach to addressing this National Standard is to plan a unit where evaluation is the primary objective. What follows are sample lessons for use in planning a music critics unit. This unit has been successfully completed with a wide variety of musical examples, and has also been used as a tool for team teaching with language-arts teachers.

Objectives:
- Students will learn about the career of music criticism.
- Students will distinguish between description and evaluation (or, if you prefer, fact and opinion).
- Students will write a critique of a song of their choice.
- Students will support their evaluations with musical terms.

Materials: Paper and pencil, CD player, several listening selections in a variety of styles (no more than three minutes in length), chart tablet or large paper, markers, computer and projector or overhead projector, examples of music criticism from newspapers, magazines, and/or the Internet.

LESSON 1: DISTINGUISHING BETWEEN DESCRIPTION AND EVALUATION

1. Play a listening selection, and ask students to write down what they hear.
2. On large paper, create a chart (see table 7.1). Ask students to tell you what they heard, and write their ideas in the appropriate column. As in the sample, leave a space in the corresponding column for each entry. If there are not a lot of responses or if you feel it would be helpful, play the recording again.
3. Ask students to explain the difference between a *description* (statement of fact) and an *evaluation* (statement of opinion). Together, rephrase each statement to fit the corresponding column (see table 7.2).

LESSON 2: READING A MUSIC CRITIQUE

1. Discuss with students the career of being a music critic. Explore what abilities a music critic should have, such as good listening skills, a large vocabulary, writing talent, and knowledge of repertoire.

Table 7.1

Description	Evaluation
Flute, piano, trombone.	
	Too fast.
No words.	
Rondo form.	
	Couldn't hear the flute clearly.

Table 7.2

Description	Evaluation
Flute, piano, trombone.	There weren't enough instruments
Tempo: allegro.	Too fast.
No words.	I like songs with lyrics better.
Rondo form.	Nice contrast between A, B, and C sections.
Trombone was louder than the flute	Couldn't hear the flute clearly.

2. Distribute examples of music criticism from newspapers, magazines, and/ or the Internet. Ask students to skim the articles and circle or list all the adjectives they find. (Yes, you'll probably have to remind them what an adjective is.)

3. Using chart tablet or large paper, make a list of a representative sample of the adjectives the students circled. Label each adjective with a *D* for "description" or an *E* for "evaluation." If necessary, ask a student to read the adjective in context to determine if it's a description or an evaluation. Explain that good music critics include both description and evaluation in their writing.

4. Ask students to skim an article again to look for one positive and one negative statement, and select students to read their examples to the class. Explain that good music critics also include both positive and negative evaluations in their writing.

LESSON 3: USING MUSIC VOCABULARY

1. Choose a listening example for this lesson that your students have probably not heard before. (You might try "She's Too Good for Me," recorded by Sting. It has a clear ABA form with strong contrast between A and B.) During the first listening, have students write down what they hear. However, they should limit themselves to descriptive statements only. Choose students to share their ideas with the class.
2. During a second listening, ask students to add to their list of descriptive statements, as well as jotting down a few evaluative statements. Discuss these ideas as a class.
3. Make a list, on large paper or the chalkboard, of the elements of music. (There are varying accepted lists of the elements of music. Use the terms that you have taught your students.) Choose volunteers to share their descriptions of the listening selection using music terms, and add those answers to the list. Your list might look something like table 7.3.
4. Next, add another column to your chart for evaluation. As a class, fill in the column using appropriate terminology, such as in table 7.4.
5. Save the charts for use during the next lesson.

LESSON 4: WRITING MUSIC CRITICISM AS A CLASS

1. Post the charts from the last lesson, and ask students to refresh their memories by reading the chart silently while listening to the selection again.
2. Ask students if any descriptions or evaluations should be added.
3. Together, choose a rating system for evaluating the song (e.g., two thumbs up, four stars out of five). Ask each student to privately rate the song, and then compare the ratings across the class.
4. (If available, this next step is much more efficient with a computer and projector; however, an overhead projector, a large sheet of paper, or even a chalkboard will do.) With one person (probably you) designated as the recorder, have the class write a critique of the listening selection together. An appropriate format might be as follows:
   - Paragraph 1: Introduce the song and the artist, including only descriptive statements.
   - Paragraph 2: Evaluate the song, referring to the charts from the last lesson, as well as the list of adjectives generated in lesson 2. Be specific, and include both positive and negative statements.
   - Paragraph 3: Summarize and rate the song using the rating system agreed upon by the class.

Table 7.3

Element of Music	Description
Rhythm	Lots of syncopation. Repeated rhythm patterns.
Tempo	A section is allegro. B section is andante.
Dynamics	A section is mostly forte. B section is mostly mezzo piano.
Timbre	One male voice. Drums, guitar, keyboards.
Melody	Mostly moves by steps and repeats.
Harmony	Solo voice only—no harmony.
Form	ABA form with coda.

5. Print copies of the critique for the class, or make a large copy to post in the classroom.
6. For the next lesson, students should come prepared with the title and artist of a song they wish to critique. A printout of the lyrics is especially helpful.

LESSON 5: WRITING MUSIC CRITICISM ALONE

1. Distribute copies of the critique written by the class in the last lesson, prominently post a large copy in the classroom, or project the critique on a screen. Read it together, reminding students of the difference between description and evaluation, the importance of including positive and negative evaluations, the use of music vocabulary, and the three-paragraph format. Students may use the class critique as a guide for writing their own.

Table 7.4

Element of Music	Description	Evaluation
Rhythm	Lots of syncopation. Repeated rhythm patterns.	Repeated rhythm patterns encourage the listener to sing along.
Tempo	A section is allegro. B section is andante.	Strong tempo contrast grabs the listener's attention.
Dynamics	A section is mostly forte. B section is mostly mezzo piano.	The A section is too loud; perhaps mezzo forte would work better.
Timbre	One male voice. Drums, guitar, keyboards.	Maybe add brass instruments in the A section.
Melody	Mostly moves by steps and repeats.	Not much melodic interest.
Harmony	Solo voice only—no harmony.	Harmony would sound better in the A section.
Form	ABA form with coda.	Repeating A at the end works well here.

2. The culminating activity for this unit is for each student to write a critique of a song of his or her choice, using the format described above. (See figure 7.1 for sample directions.) At this point, explain the project to the students, assign a due date, and discuss how their work will be graded. Many states have adopted a rubric for grading writing on state assessments. Consult a language arts teacher in your school to adapt the rubric for this project.

It is your prerogative as the teacher to determine how much work should be accomplished during class and how much at home. You might consider

Choose a song to critique. Listen to it carefully several times, and evaluate its effectiveness. Write a piece of music criticism that expresses your evaluation of the song you chose.

Your writing should include the following:

- At least 3 paragraphs, including introduction, body, and conclusion;
- The title of the song and the name of either the composer or the artist who recorded it;
- A description of the song: instrumentation, tempo, form, voicing, and so on;
- An evaluation of the song. You must include at least one positive and negative statement. Be specific and respectful in your evaluation.

Figure 7.1. Writing Assignment: Music Criticism

requiring students to submit a rough draft for your review, or perhaps plan for peer review during class time. It is also a good idea to coordinate your efforts with the language-arts teacher; this might be an assignment that is completed in both classes and graded by both teachers.

FINAL STEP: PUBLICATION

Your students' best efforts are now ready to be showcased. Finished products can be read aloud to the class, displayed on a bulletin board, published in a school newsletter, or posted on the school website. Be sure to obtain parental permission when students' names are published.

During the course of this unit, students have learned to evaluate music performances, gained experience with the career of music criticism, and reviewed music vocabulary. Your kids will be thrilled at having had a chance to express their opinions and choose their own listening selections, while you will enjoy the learning that has taken place. And your administrator will be impressed with the opportunity you've created for strengthening students' writing skills and producing work that can be showcased publicly. All in all, not a bad day's work!

CHAPTER 8

National Standard 8

National Standard 8: Understanding relationships between music, the other arts, and disciplines outside the arts.

(Consortium of National Arts
Education Associations, 1994, 45)

In the Sunday comics, when cartoon characters discover something new, they are depicted with a light bulb above the head. Some may refer to this as an "aha" moment or perhaps as an *epiphany*, while others may be inspired to shout "Eureka!" Regardless of its name, it can be an inspiration for the one lucky enough to experience it. When I was in high school, I can recall just such a moment. It was the moment when I discovered that the Romans I was learning about in Latin class were the same Romans I heard about on Sunday mornings in Bible study.

In retrospect, the truly amazing part of this discovery was that it took me so long to make it. As a reasonably intelligent child who loved reading and learning, it seems that I should have noticed the connection long before. The teacher in me looks back and wonders why I didn't notice that the word "Romans" was being used in more than one context. Why did it seem like such a surprise?

The truth is that I was probably not unique. Many students do not naturally make connections between things they learn in different places, and middle school students are no exception. (Perhaps this is why adolescents who are taught to pick up after themselves at home seem to have no idea they should do the same at school.) If we want our students to cross the space between two separate pieces of knowledge, we will have to build them a bridge, or better yet, supply the materials and show them how to build their own.

The purpose of National Standard 8 is to show students that music is intricately connected to other areas of learning. For all the students who ask, "Why do I have to learn about music?" or "What does this have to do with the real world?" this standard provides an answer. Rather than being an isolated strand, music is part of a complex web of human understanding. To fully understand the discipline of music, our students need to see how it is irrevocably affected by mathematical principles, scientific laws, the creative process, and artistic expression.

Perhaps this is an appropriate time to discuss what National Standard 8 includes and what it does not. Helping students discover that the duration of a half note is half the duration of a whole note requires mention of fractions. This demonstrates the relationship between music and math, and as such is part of this standard. However, singing a song about fractions for the *sole* purpose of memorizing math facts does not have much to do with teaching music. That is not to say that isn't a useful activity; but let's be clear on what the objective of this activity is, and what it is not.

The connections must be made for the purpose of enhancing the students' understanding of music; if there is no music learning in the activity, then it probably belongs outside of the music classroom. While it may on occasion be necessary to remind administrators and policy makers that music can positively impact standardized test scores, our primary objective is always to teach music to students.

Let's also take a moment to acknowledge that as music educators, we are not experts in every subject. This is a good opportunity for us to reach out to our colleagues to further our own understanding. Although our fellow teachers are as busy as we are, I have yet to meet one who wasn't willing to talk about ways that our subject areas are connected. These conversations are a win-win situation; while we learn more about other subject areas, our colleagues learn more about music as well, and that can only benefit our students.

In this chapter, we will explore some ways to connect music with the other arts and disciplines. For convenience, the ideas are organized according to the related subject area. The chapter will conclude with a unit about music careers, with special attention to "combination careers" where knowledge of music and another subject is required. You will notice that connections with social studies and history are not included here, as they are a primary focus of the next chapter.

Reading

If we do our jobs well, eventually our students won't need us anymore. After all, if students have a strong enough foundation, there are many things about music that they can learn on their own. However, they won't be able to learn about music through written text unless they understand the basic vocabulary that musicians use every day.

One way to build students' vocabulary is to create a "word wall" by posting words and definitions in the classroom. You might also invite students to create drawings that represent the words you've included. Start with the elements and principles of music (*pitch, melody, duration, rhythm,* etc.), add Italian terms as you teach them (*coda, fortissimo, andante,* and so forth), and don't forget the words that musicians take for granted but our students might not know (e.g., *ensemble, unison,* and *finale*). Aside from the obvious benefits to students, it is also a useful reminder to parents, colleagues, and administrators that music is a discipline with its own set of knowledge.

Sometimes students are more motivated to read about music if they are looking for a specific piece of information. Some are especially intrigued if it is called a "challenge question" and they receive extra credit for finding the answer. For example, students might be asked to discover two composers who were born the same year as Handel, or the names of three stringed instruments from Japan, or five facts about a particular jazz artist. They will have to discover the answer to the challenge by finding a resource (probably on the Internet) and reading it. They are not reading for the sake of reading, which is a guaranteed method of making them not want to do it, but are instead reading to find a specific piece of information.

It can also be helpful to introduce key pieces of literature that support and enhance students' understanding of a composer or musical era. For example, as suggested earlier, a unit about Woody Guthrie might be introduced by reading aloud the first chapter of *Grapes of Wrath* by John Steinbeck. It contains a vivid description of a dust storm such as the one described by Guthrie is his song "So Long," which could be taught during the course of the unit. (The Steinbeck-Guthrie connection is a strong one, as they lived during the same time period, and Guthrie was even influenced to write songs based on the Tom Joad character from Steinbeck's novel.)

And for those days when you and your students need a little bit of quiet time, you might consider collecting music magazines and short books for the purpose of silent reading. Allow students to choose reading material from your collection, and plan for 10–15 minutes of independent reading. Be sure to include text at a variety of reading levels to accommodate students with special needs, and be on the lookout for books in languages other than English. Just like their younger counterparts, middle school students still enjoy books with colorful illustrations.

In addition to using written text to deepen students' understanding of music, we can make an important connection in this area through song lyrics. Many general music teachers are accomplished vocalists in their own right, and as such are well aware that an expressive performance of a song is dependent on a thorough understanding of its lyrics. Here is a wonderful opportunity to point out examples of alliteration, simile, metaphor, and imagery. Or perhaps an analysis of the rhyme scheme might be helpful, along with a comparison to the letters musicians use to represent the form of a song. Ask students to determine if the song is expressed through first-, second-, or third-person point of view, and discuss whether the composer's purpose in writing the song was to persuade, inform, or entertain.

Writing

The ability to express oneself in writing is an important life skill, and there are many ways to incorporate it into the general music classroom. You might consider having students keep a journal in which they write about the music they hear and answer thought-provoking questions. To encourage students to express themselves without the pressure of needing to get the "right" answer, ask lots of open-ended opinion questions. This is also a good opportunity to include higher-order thinking skills; try to use key words like *compare, interpret, analyze, connect,* or *predict.* However, be aware that journal-writing activities can be time-consuming; be sure you have enough time for writing and follow-up discussion. Here are some examples of writing prompts that are appropriate for journal activities:

Why do musicians write down their music?
Describe the music that is part of your family's holiday celebration (any holiday).
How can you take care of your voice, and why is it important to do so?
What are five things you can't do without your voice? Make a list or draw pictures.
If you could learn to play any instrument, which one would you choose, and why?
What is your favorite song, and why?
Who is your favorite contemporary recording artist, and why?
Why do you think advertisers include music in television and radio commercials?
Can listening to a particular kind of music affect your emotions? Why or why not?
What is the purpose of a school song?
How are writing a song and painting a picture similar?
Name as many places as you can think of where you heard music during the last twenty-four hours.

Displaying or publishing exemplary written responses can be an effective way to share students' thinking with the school community. For example, a bulletin board might feature photographs of jazz legends, along with students' writing about where they see improvisation in the real world. Or pieces of music criticism from the music critics unit (see chapter 7) could be published in the school newspaper. Written work could be added to students' music portfolios to share with parents during report-card conferences. Be sure to check your district's policies about publishing students' names and work, and get any required permission from parents and students beforehand.

In addition to using writing activities to encourage thinking and expression, there is another important connection to be made with writing. The process that students use when creating written text is remarkably similar to that for music composition. Although your district may use different terminology, my students are very familiar with words like *prewrite, edit, revise,* and *publish.* Simply using this vocabulary when explaining a composition project enables students to activate the prior knowledge they have about the creative process. Remind students that just like they must edit and revise a writing assignment before making a final draft, they should do the same with a musical composition, making changes until they are satisfied with the final product.

Science

Sometimes the student who enjoys science class (where facts are observable and measurable) finds it hard to relate to music class (where the less-tangible medium of sound is the focus). However, there are proven scientific laws that govern the way sound is produced, and by understanding these principles, much can be understood about our discipline. At the beginning of a unit about musical instruments, consider reminding students of three facts:

1. Sound is caused by vibration.
2. If you stop the vibration, you stop the sound.
3. The longer the area that vibrates, the slower the vibration and the lower the pitch.

There are lots of engaging ways to demonstrate these principles. I have yet to find a class that wasn't enthralled with tuning forks; even the most recalcitrant of adolescents will want to hold one and make it vibrate. Students can learn the meaning of the frequency numbers imprinted on each tuning fork, and discover the mathematical relationship between the frequencies of notes that are an octave apart.

The three facts listed above were chosen to lead naturally to other concepts. For example, before students participate in playing piano, they might first learn about the parts of the instrument. If sound is caused by vibration, something must be vibrating (the strings) and something must cause the vibration (the hammers). When a finger is lifted off the key, the sound stops; something must have stopped the vibration (the dampers). And since each key plays a different pitch, the strings must be different sizes. Open up the instrument and show students how the parts work, and help them discover for themselves how the damper pedal allows the vibrations to continue even when the key is released. For all the students who want to take things apart to find out how they work, music class has just become very interesting.

Of course, these facts are also applicable to other areas, such as a study of how the human voice works, or a discussion of how the instruments of the orchestra are classified, or how the Japanese koto is similar to and different from a harp. If time allows, help students discover the answers to other questions about acoustics: Does sound travel more easily through a solid, a liquid, or a gas? What does the sound post of a violin do, and why is there a round hole in the center of a guitar? How do architects design a concert hall so that as much sound as possible travels to the audience?

Mathematics

For many years, my next-door neighbor at school was a sixth grade math teacher, and she used to share with me the difficulty her students were having with the concept of ratios. After one of our conversations, I began to think about the mathematical ratios represented in music. Aside from the ratios represented by frequencies, as mentioned above, there are also the relationships between the beat values of a note when the bottom number of the time signature changes. Couldn't those numbers be represented in a ratio chart like the one my colleague was using with her students? When receiving information in a familiar format, students found the concept of time signatures to be easier to understand, and if they happened to have made progress in math class too, so much the better.

Ratios are also at work in the division and subdivision of the beat. Try asking students to clap four-beat measures as follows: a whole note, then two half notes, four quarter notes, eight eighth notes, and sixteen sixteenth notes. Help students represent the relationships between each measure as a ratio.

It is interesting to note that both musicians and mathematicians are experts at discerning patterns. Anytime students are led to discover an ostinato, sequence, chord progression, or recurring theme, mathematical principles are at work as well.

There are also songs that lend themselves well to math challenges. For example, many students enjoy singing "Seasons of Love" by Jonathan Larson, from the musical *Rent*. The song begins with the number 525,600, the number of minutes in a year. When students are challenged to calculate that figure for themselves (with pencil and paper only), they more fully understand the lyrics of the song. Another song with a fun math problem is "The Twelve Days of Christmas." If one were to actually receive all the gifts, how many separate items would that be? (It's more than you think!)

And if this is all Greek to you, your math colleagues are likely to be flattered and intrigued by the chance to explore the connection between math and music—go ask them.

The Arts

Expressing oneself through the arts is a basic human instinct, although it can take place through a variety of media. When helping students understand the connection between music and other art forms, perhaps the place to start is with a basic question: "Why do human beings create art?" Students are likely to come up with a variety of answers—to express feelings, to entertain, to preserve culture, to practice religion, to communicate, and to make money. Although one artist may choose to compose a song, another to paint a landscape, and a third to write a poem, they are all compelled to create art for remarkably similar reasons. This phenomenon is worth exploring with students.

One way to look at this is to focus on common vocabulary. Here are some examples of words that have meaning in more than one art form: *line, texture, form, color, genre, improvisation, style, rhythm, shape, balance, contrast*, and *repetition*. How many ways, and in how many art forms, can you and your students apply these terms? Do the terms mean exactly the same thing in each of the arts? Why do different media have words in common?

There are many other points of intersection between music and the other arts. For example, to more fully understand the work of a particular composer, students might look at visual artwork of the same period. When studying the music of Claude Debussy, it might be helpful for students to look at the work of Claude Monet and other impressionist painters. The compositions of J. S. Bach might make more sense when compared with baroque architectural styles. And the stretching of boundaries that has occurred in the last century of music history might find parallels in the abstract paintings of the same time period.

Some forms of creative expression depend on more than one of the arts for their very existence. For example, let's take a look at the ballet *The Three-Cornered*

Hat. Based on a story by Pedro Antonio de Alarcón, the music was composed by Manuel de Falla, with Pablo Picasso completing the sets and Leonide Massine creating the choreography. The worlds of writing, music, art, and dance meet in one coherent creation, where the whole is more than the sum of its parts. In similar ways, opera and musicals can also showcase how artists collaborate to tell a story to an audience. (And although our students may not want to admit it, they do love a good story.)

One advantage of working with this age level is that adolescents have not quite decided what they can and can't do; the inhibitions that keep an adult from taking the risk of creative expression are not yet fully established. Planning activities in which creativity is encouraged in more than one medium is another way to help students build a connection between the various arts. Students could create visual artwork inspired by the strong imagery in Guthrie's "This Land is Your Land." Small groups could create movements that represent the difference between staccato and legato. A scene from an opera or musical could be staged by a class, complete with sets and costumes.

Careers Unit

Although the word *career* does not occur anywhere in the National Standards, there are many compelling reasons for including the study of music careers in general music, even as early as middle school. For one thing, the school community should be made aware that there are many ways to make a living in the music world, both on and off the stage. General music is not the impractical class that many perceive it to be, and helping students discover their vocation is as important in music as it is in any other subject. Since many successful musicians begin their training at an early age, the earlier such a vocation in music is determined, the better.

But in a broader sense, a focus on career preparation makes a lot of sense for middle school students. They are at the perfect age to explore their options and interests, without the pressure of needing to make an immediate choice. In addition, some at-risk students have a rather unclear sense of "future." They sometimes need to be reminded that their actions today can create or eliminate opportunities for tomorrow, and instruction about careers can be an important way to teach this life lesson.

What follows is a description of the careers unit from my own classroom. In this unit, students learn common vocabulary, as well as specific information about several careers. Feel free to choose the careers that interest you and your students, but be sure to focus on "combination careers" in which knowledge of music and one other subject area is necessary for success. As always, the activities may need to be modified to fit your specific situation and the needs of your students.

ACTIVITY 1: VOCABULARY

Materials: Paper and pencil, chalkboard.
Time: 5–10 minutes.
Objective: Students will describe the meaning of vocabulary words relating to college study.

At the beginning of any unit about music careers, it is helpful to begin with a short vocabulary lesson. Students are not always familiar with these words, and, quite frankly, I'm not sure I was at this age either! Some important words to include in this lesson are *SAT*; *associate's*, *bachelor's*, and *master's* degrees; *full-time* versus *part-time* college study; *two-year* and *four-year* colleges; *certification*; and *internship*. Present the information in the method that is comfortable to you and familiar to your students, although students should take notes on the material for reference later on in the unit.

ACTIVITY 2: WHAT DO WE WANT TO KNOW?

Materials: Paper and pencil, chalkboard or chart paper.
Time: 10–15 minutes.
Objective: Students will discuss what they would like to learn about music careers, and create a chart for recording the information.

Give students about five minutes to create a list of things they would like to know about careers in music. At your discretion, students may work individually or in pairs. Once most of the student lists have at least five items, choose a student to record ideas on the chalkboard or chart paper, and ask students to share their ideas with the class. (Keep a copy of the responses for use in the next activity.) Here are some sample student responses: Is a college degree required? What special skills are needed? Where would a person with this career work? What are the responsibilities of a person in this career? What would a typical day be like? You may wish to guide students away from conversations about salary, as the pay scale for a particular career is likely to change by the time they enter the work force.

When a complete list has been written on the board, help students determine which ideas could be placed together in the same category. Work toward

Table 8.1

Name of Career	Preparation	Description	Location	Related Field

three or four categories of information by combining or eliminating ideas. When consensus has been reached, have each student create a chart for recording information. (See table 8.1 for an example.)

The last category, "related field," is important to include in the chart. It is here that students will make note of the related subject area for this career. For example, a recording executive needs to have knowledge of music as well as an understanding of business principles in order to be successful.

ACTIVITY 3: INTERVIEWING A MUSIC PROFESSIONAL

Materials: Pen or pencil; chalkboard notes and student charts from previous lesson.

Time: 10–15 minutes.

Objective: Students will interview a music professional and enter information on a chart.

By now you're probably wondering, "Where am I supposed to get a professional musician to visit my class?" Well, that's easy—it's you, and you're already there! Have students write "music educator" in the column marked "name of career." Choose a student or students to conduct the interview, using the questions that were generated from activity 2. All you have to do is answer the questions. When the interview is finished, ask students to share the information they wrote on their charts, and fill in anything that is missing or incomplete. Be sure that students have entered "education" as the Related Field. This is your opportunity to check that all students understand how to take notes on the chart, as they will need to know what to do in the next activity.

ACTIVITY 4–5: THE "ROTATING FOLDERS" ACTIVITY

Materials: Pen or pencil; charts from previous activities; eight manila file folders; eight sets of information about each of four music careers, such as music therapist, sound engineer, recording executive, and disc jockey.
Time: Two sessions of about 30 minutes each.
Objective: Students will read information about four careers in music and enter information on a chart.

This activity requires some preparation before the students enter the class. First, arrange the seats to allow for eight groups of four students each. Decide if you will assign students to groups or allow them to choose for themselves. (Feel free to use fewer or smaller groups. A class size of 32 is very typical for my school, so I use eight groups of four students.)

Next, write "music therapist" on the front of two of the file folders. In each of the two folders, place four sets of information about that career. In a similar fashion, create two folders for each of the other careers. Because you have created duplicate folders, two groups will be working on the same information at the same time.

When students are seated and ready to begin, give each group a folder. Tell students that they have ten minutes to look through the material and make notes on their charts. Remind them that they are allowed to write on their charts, but should not make any marks on the folders or the information inside the folders. While they are working, you will probably need to circulate among the groups to provide guidance and to minimize unrelated conversations.

After ten minutes has passed, rotate the folders to the next group. (It is *much* easier to move the folders than it is to move the students.) Remind students that they have ten minutes to follow the same procedure with their new folders. When time is up, collect all materials in preparation for the next session.

In my experience, students will work quite productively through two rotations in a given class period, but begin to lose their concentration after that. For this reason, you may wish to have groups complete the other two folders during the next class period. Keep in mind that students will need to work with the same groups for both sessions, so make a quick list of group members. If your students are very motivated and focused, it may work to have them complete all four folders on the same day.

ACTIVITY 6: COMPARING NOTES

Note: This activity may be completed at the end of the previous activity.
Materials: Completed charts from the previous activities, pen or pencil.

Time: About 10 minutes.

Objective: Students will discuss information from their charts, and fill in missing or incomplete information.

When all the groups have completed all four folders, it is helpful to discuss the information that was gathered in a large-group setting. During the course of the conversation, you will be able to assess if students fully understand the material, or if you will need to do some reteaching. When all is said and done, each student should have a chart with information about five careers in music (music educator from activity 3 and four careers from activity 4–5). It is up to you to decide how your students will be graded for their participation in this unit—you might administer a test, or perhaps just award points for a completed chart. This unit could also be followed by an at-home research project about another career in music.

In this chapter, we've discussed some ways to help students build a bridge between music and other subject areas. These ideas were designed to incorporate reading, writing, mathematics, science, and the arts in ways that enhance musical learning. These strategies may lead you to discover your own ways to fulfill this important standard. In the meantime, don't be alarmed if words like "aha" or "eureka" have been heard in your classroom; and if your building administrators want to know why there are light bulbs hovering over your students' heads, just direct them to National Standard 8!

CHAPTER 9

National Standard 9

National Standard 9: Understanding music in relation to history and culture.

(Consortium of National Arts
Education Associations, 1994, 45)

Adolescents are notoriously self-centered. Their "world" is anything that directly affects them, and "history" begins on their date of birth. From the point of view of an average middle school student, events that happened centuries ago and an ocean away are not only irrelevant, but essentially nonexistent. In some ways we can hardly blame them: such information may not seem terribly helpful to a child trying to survive report cards, peer pressure, puberty, and a locker that won't open. And those are the lucky ones—add in the very real traumas of depression, child abuse, neighborhood violence, or poverty, and we should not be surprised that the events of the past don't seem to hold much interest for our students.

And yet, it can be amazingly comforting to realize that people from all time periods and cultures have struggled to survive and thrive within their own reality, just like we do. Music has an unique ability to serve as a historical/cultural record while simultaneously expressing the innermost feelings of the ones who created it. To open our students' eyes to the music embedded in history and culture is to give them a lens through which their own lives take on a new clarity.

This presents us with both a challenge and an opportunity. Can we make music from the past relevant to today's youth? Can we present music of other cultures accurately and sensitively? Can we introduce composers who died many years ago and make them come alive to our students? Can we build strong connections to the world outside our classroom doors? Yes, of course we can; and, furthermore, we can do this in a way that is engaging and motivating to our students.

In this chapter, you will find descriptions of several units of study that attempt to make a connection between music, history, and culture. It is worth noting that other standards can also be addressed during these lessons. In order to fully explore a musical theme, it helps to sing, play and listen; occasionally other art forms and disciplines can be included as well. Please note that the intent is not to present an exhaustive resource for thematic units, but instead to offer some examples as a place to start. Perhaps in reading through these ideas, you will be inspired to modify them or develop your own in order to best meet the needs of your students.

You will notice that multicultural resources do not receive much mention in the examples that follow. It must be stated, in the strongest possible terms, that National Standard 9 cannot be fully met without the inclusion of music from many cultures. However, there are many available recordings, books, and lessons compiled by music educators and musicologists with a great deal of expertise and experience. To try to present such a topic in a portion of a single chapter would be a great disservice.

Musicians of Courage

Middle school, not to mention life, can be a scary place. Every day our students run the gauntlet through crowded hallways, noisy cafeterias, and pressure-filled classrooms. Although they might not choose the word "courage" to describe it, they certainly understand the effort it takes to face each day. It's interesting to think about situations in which composers had to use courage to overcome an obstacle and continue their work. How might this theme allow us to view musical creativity in a new light, and perhaps find parallels in our own lives?

Although there are many composers to choose from, our unit begins with Igor Stravinsky, whose composition *Rite of Spring* caused a riot during its premiere. Great courage must have been required to continue composing the music he felt inspired to create, despite such a violent reaction from the public. Many students enjoy the unusual rhythms and strong dissonances contained in the piece.

The second composer in the series is Duke Ellington. It's important for students to know about the difficulties he faced as an African American living in a segregated country, and the dignity and courage he displayed throughout his lifetime. Listening to several of his songs could even lay the groundwork for a jazz unit later in the semester.

Last, students will learn about Pete Seeger, for whom music continues to be a way to express his engagement with the world and its challenges. It could not have been easy to show courage in the face of political oppression, and to continue to write music that shines with the sincerity of his beliefs. It's an interesting challenge to present his recordings to students who may prefer rap, R & B, and reggaeton.

As it happens, all three composers lived during the same century and spent at least part of their lives living in the United States, yet the music they wrote is vastly different. This presents an opportunity for students to think about the contrasts between them. In order to develop the theme, two lessons are planned for each composer. The first presents biographical information, and the second allows for interactive listening experiences. The unit concludes with an opportunity for students to make comparisons between the three composers.

When introducing a composer to our students, it's sometimes helpful to avoid the "read and answer questions" strategy, as the students who receive special services may have difficulty with reading comprehension. Presenting the biographical lessons in a conversational tone can help the composer come alive in the classroom, and expecting students to take notes of key words and phrases keeps them engaged and attentive.

One way to present biographical information is to create a computer slideshow for each composer, containing photographs and the information that students are required to know. Presentations can be created easily, and it's a great way to display images; as an added bonus, students are more motivated to pay attention than with traditional chalkboard notes. If you are unfamiliar with using slideshow software programs, talk to your school's technology coordinator for a quick lesson. Your school may even have a computer projector that you can borrow for your classroom.

The listening lessons focus on short excerpts of several parts of Stravinsky's *Rite of Spring*, and a few songs written by Ellington and Seeger using their own recordings. We're aiming for a brief introduction to the music, rather than an in-depth analysis that may not hold the students' interest.

Here is an outline of material that may be included in the biographical and listening lessons. For convenience, the words in italics represent the notes students are expected to make, and words in parentheses are some thoughts about how to communicate these ideas to the students.

LESSON 1: STRAVINSKY'S LIFE

1882–1971.
(Ask students to think of world events that occurred during Stravinsky's lifetime.)
Born in Russia.

(Now is a good time to talk about the upheaval in Russia during Stravinsky's early years, which included events such as Bloody Sunday and the Revolution of 1905.)

Pianist and composer.

(Of course, students should know the skills for which Stravinsky is best known.)

Worked with Diaghilev and Picasso.

(Ask students to name some of the careers involved in successfully producing a ballet, and then explain Sergei Diaghilev's and Pablo Picasso's roles in *Rite of Spring*. There is a wonderful caricature of Stravinsky drawn by Picasso that is available online; it makes a good addition to a slideshow presentation. It is also interesting to show an image of Picasso's *Three Musicians*.)

Lived in Russia, Switzerland, France, and the United States.

(Students who were not born in the United States may be able to relate to Stravinsky's difficulty returning to his homeland of Russia during times of war.)

The ballet "Rite of Spring" caused a riot.

(Ask students how they would feel if the music they'd worked hard to create was booed by an audience. Then describe the event as vividly as possible, stressing Stravinsky's courage and determination to be true to his musical vision in spite of the public outcry.)

LESSON 2: STRAVINSKY'S MUSIC

Rite of Spring is a hefty piece of music; an entire semester could be spent on this piece alone, so our goal here is a brief introduction to the music. When presenting this lesson, begin with a description of the story and a list of the titles of each episode. Choose a listening question for students to consider while hearing a minute or two from the beginning of selected episodes. Switch questions often to keep students engaged. Here are a few that might work for your students:

1. What instruments do you hear? Why do you think Stravinsky chose those instruments?
2. Does Stravinsky use the same tempo and dynamics throughout, or are there changes? Why do you think he does that?
3. What emotions are conveyed in this section?
4. What do you think Stravinsky was trying to communicate to the audience?
5. Does the title of this episode match the music? Why or why not?
6. Do you think the audience was right to react so violently to this piece?
7. Since this piece is a ballet, what style of dancing would match the music you hear?

8. What costumes, sets, or scenery might fit the music and the story of this ballet?

LESSON 3: ELLINGTON'S LIFE

1899–1974.

(Ask students to compare the life spans of Stravinsky and Ellington. Also, be sure to talk about the major events in the civil rights movement that occurred during Ellington's life.)

Born in Washington, D.C.

(It was here that Ellington learned to play the piano; one of Ellington's first bands was called "The Washingtonians.")

Nickname inspired by elegant clothing and manners.

(Many contemporary recording artists use nicknames, and students can certainly relate to giving nicknames to their friends. It may be fun to discuss other jazz musicians who have notable nicknames.)

Pianist and composer.

(Be sure that students make the connection with Stravinsky. Mention to students that although the two men had similar talents, their music is very different.)

Often composed for specific players.

(Ellington's composition "Concerto for Cootie" is an appropriate example.)

Worked with Billy Strayhorn.

(It's interesting to note that the signature song of Ellington's orchestra, "Take the 'A' Train," was actually written by Strayhorn. Tell your students that when they win *Jeopardy!* with this question, you expect them to give you credit.)

Performed around the world.

(It's important for students to know that Ellington's success was not limited to the United States; his performances abroad were highly acclaimed.)

Successful despite discrimination.

(Students may be interested in seeing a photograph of Duke Ellington accepting the Presidential Medal of Freedom from President Nixon in 1969, which is available online. This demonstrates the level of success he achieved in spite of adversity.)

LESSON 4: ELLINGTON'S MUSIC

Ellington wrote many songs during his lifetime, so there are plenty to choose from. In planning this listening lesson, you will probably want to limit yourself to songs that are between two and four minutes in length, so that students can have the opportunity to hear several songs before they lose interest. Students will be most appropriately introduced to Ellington's style by using only original recordings, rather than covers by other artists. (Although a compare/contrast exercise of two versions of an Ellington classic might be a fun extension to this unit.)

"It Don't Mean a Thing (If It Ain't Got That Swing)"
(One of Ellington's best known songs, some students are familiar with it without
    being aware of who wrote it. There is a wonderful recording with Ellington
    and Ella Fitzgerald that your students will enjoy.)
"Koko"
(Ellington wrote this piece in commemoration of the drum ceremonies in
    Congo Square, New Orleans, a cultural connection that it is important to
    share with students. See the references for Luvenia George's terrific lesson
    plan for introducing this piece (1999b).
"Take the 'A' Train"
(Since this song is widely used in soundtracks of TV shows and movies, it would be
    nice for students to be able to recognize the melody when they hear it in other
    places. Have students read or listen to the lyrics of this song to discover how
    the "A" train in the New York City subway system provides transportation to
    the Sugar Hill community in Harlem, and discuss Strayhorn's and Ellington's
    places in the Harlem Renaissance. After listening to the song, see if students
    can put into words the pervasive sense of optimism and excitement.)
"Daybreak Express"
(A great example of program music, this piece lends itself to a "guess the title"
    game. If you introduce "Take the 'A' Train" first, your students may guess
    that title for this piece; remind them that the "A" train is a subway, which
    sounds different from a freight or passenger train. Help students discover
    the musical clues like the train whistle, the wheels clicking on the tracks, and
    the accelerando and rallentando of the beginning and ending. Mention to
    students that Ellington and his band frequently traveled by train, and so this
    piece demonstrates the way life experiences can be recorded in music.)

LESSON 5: SEEGER'S LIFE

Born in 1919, in New York City.
(Again, make comparisons among the lifetimes of all three composers, and be
    sure that students notice that their lives overlapped.)
Parents and stepmother were musicians.
(Seeger's stepmother was Ruth Crawford Seeger, an important composer.)

Banjo player, singer, and composer.
(The banjo may not be familiar to some students, so a photo here is helpful. Ask kids to figure out the advantages of a banjo over the piano for accompanying singing; after all, it's hard to bring a piano to a campfire or a protest rally!)
Worked for American Folk Song Archives.
(Seeger's work for the archives demonstrates his interest in music created by and for the people.)
Worked with Woody Guthrie, the Almanac Singers, and the Weavers.
(This fact may help make a connection to songs many students already know, "This Land Is Your Land" and "The Lion Sleeps Tonight.")
Politically active.
(Students need to know that Seeger expresses his political views through music. It may be helpful to mention some of the things that Seeger feels strongly about, such as the antiwar movements, civil rights, and environmental causes.)
Testified before House Un-American Activities Committee, 1955.
(Some explanation will be needed here; many students are unfamiliar with this period in our history, and are too young to remember the national fear of Communism. Stress that Seeger had the courage to hold to his beliefs and that he refused to answer questions he felt were inappropriate, despite enormous pressure to do so. You may find it interesting to read the transcript of Seeger's testimony, which is available online.)

LESSON 6: SEEGER'S MUSIC

When presenting Pete Seeger's music to students, it is important for students to hear his own voice, not merely recordings of other artists performing his work. There are many albums available, and single songs can be purchased and downloaded online. Be sure to prepare students for the difference in vocal style between Seeger and contemporary recording artists, and review your expectations for their behavior when listening to something new.

Here are examples of well-known songs that could be presented during this listening lesson, along with a few thoughts on why and how to introduce them to students. There are many other options, so feel free to make substitutions. As with Duke Ellington, the hard part is narrowing down such a long list of wonderful choices.

"We Shall Overcome"
(Although Seeger did not compose this song, he often performed it as a symbol of determination and courage during the civil rights movement. There are

many recordings available, but a live performance by Seeger would be most appropriate here. Although some students may already be able to sing along, its place in American history makes it a song everyone should know.)

"Where Have All the Flowers Gone?"

(Another iconic song, this selection shows Seeger's ability to make a statement in indirect, yet powerful ways. Spend a few moments talking to students about cause and effect; this concept is explored in other subjects in middle school. After listening to the song, help students trace the cause-and-effect series, and ask them to summarize the message Seeger is trying to convey. The storytelling quality to the song is often appealing to this age group.)

"If I Had a Hammer"

(Written by Seeger and his fellow Weaver, Lee Hays, this is a song that many students will know from elementary general music, even if perhaps they were not aware of its composers. Encourage your students to sing along with the recording.)

"You Are My Sunshine"

(Although Seeger did not write this song either, there is a very sweet recording of Seeger singing it, which students might enjoy as a "name that tune" exercise.)

CONCLUDING THE UNIT

There are several ways to wrap up the "Musicians of Courage" unit. You might have students complete a persuasive writing exercise where they each choose a contemporary recording artist who should be called a "musician of courage," and explain their choices. Or perhaps you might divide the class into three teams, to debate which of our three composers was the most courageous. A third option might be to complete a triple Venn diagram that compares and contrasts all three. Any of these options could serve as an end-of-unit assessment, in which students demonstrate their knowledge of the composers' lives and music.

Dive into Water Music

The inspiration for this unit came from an exciting opportunity to view an exhibition of student artwork. There were many compelling pieces, including several that included the element of water as a central theme. It was intriguing to think about how the theme of water is explored in other media, including music.

The result was "Dive into Water Music," a unit that includes biographical and listening lessons about three composers, all from different time periods and walks of life, and all inspired in some way by water. Students explore G. F. Handel's *Water Music*, Claude Debussy's *La Mer*, and Scott Joplin's *Cascades*. The unit concludes with a compare-and-contrast writing assignment. The lessons are very similar in structure to the "Musicians of Courage" unit detailed above.

To supplement the unit, the water theme can be continued in other parts of the general music program. Students can have fun singing water songs like "Three Little Fishies" and "Octopus's Garden," and they can learn to conduct in $\frac{4}{4}$ along with Billy Joel's "The River of Dreams." Extra credit can be awarded to any student who brings in a (school-appropriate) recording of a song that extends the theme, and student artwork makes a very nice bulletin board display.

Time-Capsule Project

Do you remember where you were in 1999? Everyone was already making plans for New Year's Eve, and the computer world was feverishly trying to solve the Y2K crisis. All of that excitement was the motivation behind plans to teach about music from the year 1000 to the present. In this unit, the millennium is divided into segments of 200 or 300 years. For each segment of history, students explore the music of one or two composers, learn some appropriate vocabulary words, and discuss events, inventions, and literature. The culminating activity is to choose items to include in a virtual time capsule.

Of course, it is not easy to decide which composers, events, and so forth should be part of the unit. It's hard to cover a thousand years of music in one semester, and every teacher will have to choose for him- or herself what should be included. Here are a few examples of the material and activities that might be included in each segment. If you begin to wonder why this composer or that event is not on the list, please remember that these are only examples, not a complete lesson plan!

1000–1299

- Learn about Guido d'Arezzo and the "Guidonian Hand."
- Sing "Ut queant laxis" and discover how it inspired solfège (Grout 1980, 59–60).
- Learn the meanings of *monophony* and *polyphony*, and listen to recorded examples of each.
- Research the Crusades, the construction of the Campanile of Pisa (also known as the Leaning Tower), and Leif Erikson's voyage to Nova Scotia.

1300–1599

- Learn about Josquin des Prez, and listen to his music.
- Use the *soggetto cavato* method to create a short melody from your name, like des Prez's Mass *Hercules Dux Ferrariae* (Grout 1980, 195).
- Find definitions for *homophony* and *Renaissance*.
- Discuss other important people and events, such as Joan of Arc, Leonardo da Vinci, William Shakespeare, Christopher Columbus, and the invention of the printing press.

1600–1799

- Learn about J. S. Bach and Franz Joseph Haydn, and listen to their music.
- Discover the meaning of *fugue, sonata, baroque,* and *classical.*
- Research the original name of the piano, and find out who invented it.
- Talk about other significant facts and people, like George Washington, Benjamin Franklin, the American and French Revolutions, and the writing of *Gulliver's Travels.*

1800–PRESENT

- Learn about Frédéric Chopin and Edgard Varèse, and listen to their music.
- Learn to play the melody of "Ode to Joy" on the piano.
- Create a melody based on a twelve-tone row.
- Look up the words *Romantic, Impressionist, dodecaphonic,* and *aleatoric.*
- Discuss important people and events, such as Mahatma Ghandi, Nelson Mandela, Martin Luther King, the Civil War, and the removal of the Berlin Wall.

The culminating project of creating a time capsule can be completed in a variety of ways. Students might work in pairs or small groups, or individual students could be assigned a certain portion to contribute to a class time capsule. This can be an at-home or in-class assignment; choose the one that will most likely yield a complete project from your students. For the computer-savvy teacher, a WebQuest could be created to help students conduct research. The final product could take a number of forms, for example, a poster or slideshow presentation. See figure 9.1 for an example of directions that might be distributed to students.

Name_____Class_____Date_____

Directions: Create your own virtual time capsule by choosing one person/item for each category. You may use the chart below to organize your thoughts. Read the rubric carefully to be sure your project is complete!

1000–1299	1300–1599
Most important musician or composition:	Most important musician or composition:
Most important artist or work of art:	Most important artist or work of art:
Most important author or piece of literature:	Most important author or piece of literature:
Most important world event:	Most important world event:
Most important invention:	Most important invention:
1600–1799	**1800–present**
Most important musician or composition:	Most important musician or composition:
Most important artist or work of art:	Most important artist or work of art:
Most important author or piece of literature:	Most important author or piece of literature:
Most important world event:	Most important world event:
Most important invention:	Most important invention:

Rubric:

20 pts. One person/item for each category (20 items total).
20 pts. The date for each item and birth/death date for each person (20 dates total).
20 pts. One picture for each time period (4 pictures total, 5 points each).
20 pts. A poster or slideshow that includes the items/people, pictures, and dates; must be neat and colorful.
20 pts. Presentation to the class; must be well-prepared and include reasons for your choices.
Total: 100 points.

Figure 9.1. Time-Capsule Project

The National Anthem Project

Many of us look back with (hopefully) fond memories on family vacations to Washington, D.C. In addition to the many monuments and museums, visitors can see the actual "broad stripes and bright stars" that made such an impression on Francis Scott Key. A short drive away is Fort McHenry in Baltimore, the location of the ramparts "o'er" which the flag was "gallantly streaming." Undoubtedly, teachers who work in the Baltimore and Washington, D.C., areas are already aware of the field-trip opportunities; but for those farther away, an online search can yield great photos and images for bulletin-board displays.

It is not necessary to offer detailed lesson plans here, as MENC has many resources available on this topic. Here are a few quick thoughts concerning activities that your students may enjoy:

- Read or sing through the original lyrics, "To Anacreon in Heaven."
- Challenge your students to draw or paint the dramatic battle.
- Select volunteers to perform the song during morning or afternoon announcements.
- Award points for accurate memorization of the lyrics, with bonus points for extra verses.
- Compare "The Star-Spangled Banner" to the national anthems from countries around the world.

This chapter has focused on planning thematic units that help students discover the connections between music, history, and culture. If the units described here are not interesting to you or appropriate for your students, there are many others to consider. How about music of the Revolutionary War, lullabies from around the world, or contemporary popular music from every continent? Or maybe number 1 hits from each decade of the last century, the role of women composers throughout time, or protest songs? We are limited only by our imagination.

If thematic units are not for you, there are other strategies that help address this standard in more subtle and less time-consuming ways. Here are a few thoughts for you to consider:

Maps: Create a bulletin board with maps of the United States and the world. When teaching about a composer or introducing a new song, label the country or region of origin.

Timelines: By taping up a long piece of black yarn or ribbon along the walls, your entire classroom can become a timeline. Help students post index cards with song titles, composers, and world events at their appropriate locations on the timeline.

Sing in original languages: As mentioned in chapter 1, when learning songs from various parts of the world, challenge students to sing in the original language.

Show and tell: Encourage students to share recordings and instruments from their families' native countries. Teach the class to ask intelligent and respectful questions about music from diverse cultural backgrounds.

Coordinate with social studies: Ask your colleagues when they will be teaching about specific world regions, and look for songs, recordings, and instruments to introduce at the appropriate times.

Give background information: Be sure to share the historical and cultural context of songs and listening lessons.

National Standard 9 provides a great opportunity for students to view both music and themselves in relation to the history and cultures of the world. For our students, their "world" now extends beyond what is right outside their front door, and "history" is now both alive and relevant. Music reflects the experiences and emotions of real people, and when students understand that, it can help them express their emotions and experiences, too.

References

Center on Education Policy. 2007. *Choices, Changes, and Challenges: Curriculum and Instruction in the NCLB Era.* Washington, DC: Author.

Conard, N., M. Malina, and S. C. Munzel. 2009. New flutes document the earliest musical tradition in southwestern Germany. *Nature* 460 (August 6): 737–40. www.nature.com/nature/journal/vaop/ncurrent/full/nature08169.html (accessed July 17, 2009).

Consortium of National Arts Education Associations. 1994. *National Standards for Arts Education.* Reston, VA: MENC.

George, L. 1999a. Duke Ellington: The man and his music. *Music Educators Journal* 85, no. 6 (May): 15–21. http://mej.sagepub.com/cgi/reprint/85/6/15 (accessed July 15, 2009).

George, L. 1999b. Sample lesson for "Koko" by Duke Ellington, at http://www.dellington .org/lessons/lesson05.html.

Gerber, T., and K. Gerrity. 2007. Principles for principals: Why music remains important in middle schools. *General Music Today* 21, no. 1 (Fall): 17–23. http://gmt.sagepub .com/cgi/reprint/21/1/17 (accessed December 29, 2009).

Grout, D. J. 1980. *A History of Western Music.* 3rd ed. New York: Norton.

Jensen, E. 2001. *Arts with the Brain in Mind.* Alexandria, VA: Association for Supervision and Curriculum Development.

Levitin, D. J. 2006. *This is Your Brain on Music.* New York: Dutton.

McAnally, E. A. 2007. Meaningful listening for middle and high school students. *Teaching Music* 15, no. 1 (August): 22–26.

Mezzacappa, D. 2005. Sixth-grade tendencies can indicate risk. *Philadelphia Inquirer.* March 17, sec. B.

Whipps, H. 2008. Cave men loved to sing. July 3, at www.livescience.com/history/080703-cave-music.html (accessed July 17, 2009).

Wilson, L. M., and H. W. Horch. 2002. Implications of brain research for teaching young adolescents. *Middle School Journal* 34, no. 1 (September): 57–61. http://www .nmsa.org/Publications/MiddleSchoolJournal/Articles/September2002/Article10/tabid/418/Default.aspx (accessed Jan. 5, 2006).

The National Standards for Music Education

1. Singing, alone and with others, a varied repertoire of music
2. Performing on instruments, alone and with others, a varied repertoire of music
3. Improvising melodies, variations, and accompaniments
4. Composing and arranging music within specified guidelines
5. Reading and notating music
6. Listening to, analyzing, and describing music
7. Evaluating music and music performances
8. Understanding relationships between music, the other arts, and disciplines outside the arts
9. Understanding music in relation to history and culture

(Consortium of National Arts Education Associations, 1994, 42–45)

Tips for Working with Adolescents

Gone are the days of being able to say, "I like how Ahmad is sitting!" and then magically seeing a classroom full of good posture. No longer will it be enough to remind students to "put on your good listening ears." The sweet smiles of kindergarten have been exchanged for the grumpy faces of the young adolescent.

However, inside the unpredictable and occasionally ornery shell lies a child who longs to be acknowledged, appreciated, and engaged. All you have to do is find a way to open the shell. But here's the catch—what works for student A on Monday will not work for student A on Tuesday, or for student B on any day of the week. You don't need a "bag of tricks"; you need a couple of suitcases full and the intuition to select the right strategy at the right moment for the right child.

For the middle school general music teacher, the skills to connect with, motivate, and manage adolescents in the classroom mark the difference between success and failure. Students are aware that a passing grade in general music class is not required for promotion to the next grade; it is easy for students to feel that this class "doesn't count" and there's no reason to work hard. And since middle school students are very creative and hate to be bored, those not occupied with productive activities will find other things to do, like entertain their classmates and harass their teachers. It is times like these that make music teachers long for elementary or high school assignments.

It is my hope that this chapter will help provide some support for middle school teachers. Of course, every teacher is different, and each must find his or her own way to make connections with students. There is no substitute for personal experience, but perhaps some of my own trial and error can be of use in your classroom. What follows are some strategies that have been useful to me while navigating the fascinating world of middle school.

Talk like an adult. Middle school students hate to be patronized, so speak with the tone of voice you would use to address an adult. When using more advanced vocabulary, try to slide in a quick definition or explanation: "Scott Joplin suffered from a *progressive* disease; his illness became worse over time."

But remember that they're still children. Just because your students want to be spoken to like adults doesn't mean that they can follow adult directions. Continue to give step-by-step directions, just like you would for younger students. You'll probably even have to tell them to put their names on the paper.

Be proactive instead of reactive. It's a horrible feeling when you don't know how to respond to a situation. You'll have to figure out a solution on the spot, with an audience of thirty adolescents who just can't wait to see if you will lose your composure. These awkward moments can be avoided by anticipating potential problems and planning for their solutions. Remind students of expectations and consequences at the beginning of the lesson, and apply the consequences consistently. Try to predict logistical problems, and adjust your plans to compensate. Ultimately, there will be fewer issues to resolve, and the solutions will already be at your fingertips.

Remember that an ounce of prevention is worth a pound of migraine medicine. Preventing an issue before it occurs will save many hours of work, so now is the time for some common sense. Two students who detest each other should not sit near one another, even if their last names are in order alphabetically. If two students need to share a piano bench, choose two girls or two boys, not one of each. Consistently enforce safety rules, and plan for safe traffic flow throughout the room. And never, ever leave students unsupervised—even the most well-behaved adolescent may have trouble with impulse control.

Consider that if you fight the small battles, you might not have to fight the war. For some students, middle school can be a time of rebellion. Young adolescents have a need to create their own identity, and to become independent from authority figures such as parents and teachers. Your students will find lots of ways to challenge you, and if you don't respond to their initial, and perhaps mild, attempts at rebellion, they may try to get your attention with more serious behavior. So don't let them slide on the small stuff—make them throw out their gum, insist on full participation, and correct them for mildly inappropriate language like "shut up." Your students have made their point by attempting these things in the first place, and you have made your point by correcting them. Now that the rebellion is over, class can begin.

Encourage appropriate self-expression. At this age, students begin to form strong opinions on a wide variety of topics that are important to them, and will not hesitate to defend their positions vehemently. A teacher who creates opportunities for students to express themselves will earn their respect, and may prevent inappropriate outbursts. Allow students to research the life of a favorite recording artist for extra credit, occasionally ask them how they feel about a listening selection (*after* they listen to it), and ask open-ended questions that encourage creative thinking. Insist that all opinions be treated with respect, both by you and by classmates. Students will feel that their views are valued, and will learn how to treat other's opinions with respect.

Find the hidden reason for misbehavior. Nothing is more embarrassing for some middle school kids than to admit that they don't know how to do something. They would rather be in trouble for breaking the rules than for being unable to complete an assignment. So be on the lookout for misbehavior that occurs during challenging activities. Be aware of your students' special needs, as well as accommodations that must be followed (such as an Individualized Education Plan), and adjust your plans accordingly. Misbehavior of this type can be minimized when students are rewarded for effort, and when directions are very clear.

Hold your ground today, and tomorrow will be better. When a student engages in unfortunate behavior, he or she may feel honor bound to continue throughout the lesson. Giving in to the teacher in front of peers is not something middle school students are likely to do. However, you must stand firm, regardless of the student's protestations. By tomorrow, the student may be able to meet your expectations without embarrassment, and perhaps he or she will feel that the rebellion is just not worth the effort.

Be aware that "free time" may be costly. You will be amazed what your students can think of to do when you don't provide something for them. The extra work required to clean up the mess and follow through on misbehavior will take much more time than the free time itself. Save yourself the aggravation and keep your students very, very busy.

Be on the lookout for "red flag" behavior. The myriad changes experienced during adolescence can cause great emotional turmoil for some students. Additionally, some middle school students have much less adult supervision outside of school hours than their younger counterparts. As a result, students who may desperately need support sometimes escape the notice of concerned adults, and they may be afraid to ask for help themselves. So be on the lookout for "red flags", such as dramatic changes in behavior, achievement, or personal appearance, or evidence of infliction of harm by self or others. Be sure to bring your concerns to the attention of your school counselor. You may just save a life.

Remember that some students play confusing roles. As they enter middle school, some students are expected to assume increasing (and in some cases inappropriate) levels of adult responsibility, such as extended care for younger siblings and lengthy periods of self-supervision. It can be very hard for them to accept autocratic authority from teachers when they answer only to themselves outside of school hours. Work *with* these students; guide, suggest, and gently steer them where they need to go. Heavy-handed bossiness will be unsuccessful.

Show sincere appreciation. Although it is no longer effective to say, "I like how Ahmad is sitting," students still want to be acknowledged when they do the right thing. Let students know when you are proud of their efforts, and be very specific. When compliments are delivered with a serious rather than a patronizing tone of voice, students will know that you mean what you say. However, these types of comments are most effective when directed to groups of students, rather than individuals.

Utilize the "hit and run" compliment. If you make a big production of complimenting the efforts of an individual student in front of peers, that student may just do the opposite to avoid being seen as a teacher's pet. Instead, speak to the student privately at the end of the lesson, then immediately send him or her to class. Deliver your congratulations quickly (that's the "hit"), and don't give the student time to react (that's the "run"). Your words are more likely to have the desired impact because the student is not put on the spot. This technique is particularly effective when the student isn't expecting a compliment: "I sensed that you really didn't feel like participating today, but I am impressed that you joined in when I reminded you a few times. I want you to know that I noticed your effort. Now, go to class."

Be aware that middle school students are like mirrors. In other words, you will get out of them what you put in. A sarcastic, impatient attitude from the teacher will yield a sullen, resentful response from the students, while an encouraging attitude from the teacher creates a positive response. An angry voice from the teacher will escalate a conflict, while a calm and firm tone of voice may de-escalate it. Admittedly, it is hard to be bombarded by middle school negativity all day and still respond positively, but the results will be worth the effort. (Do what you need to do to keep an optimistic point of view—listen to uplifting music on the way to work, read a funny book at the end of the day . . . and, of course, chocolate never hurts!)

Avoid yelling. Yes, this is a tough one, because adolescents are so very, very good at pushing our buttons. Here's the problem—the more we yell, the less our students listen. In addition, middle school students love to be entertained, and making us yell can be very amusing; they may start to instigate this reaction on purpose. Lower your voice, and speak with firm authority; your voice and your blood pressure will thank you at the end of the day.

Graciously admit when you're wrong. Teachers who hate to own up to their mistakes will have classes full of students who can't wait to prove them wrong. When an error occurs, admit it, apologize, and move on. The students who see this will become adults who can learn from their own mistakes.

Never tell them it's easy. Tell them it's hard. If students are led to believe that a task is easy but they still have trouble with it, they will become very frustrated. If they believe it's hard, any step toward the goal feels like progress.

Remember that there's a big difference between sixth grade and eighth grade. When students come to middle school in fifth or sixth grade, they have plenty of energy and enthusiasm, but need direction, structure, and attention. They need to be told when (and maybe how) to sharpen their pencils, and opening their lockers is about as easy as neurosurgery. Eighth graders, on the other hand, are very independent creatures. They don't want to be patronized, and, left to their own devices, they would sleep until noon every day. Clearly, different strategies will be needed with these very different age groups. If you expect independence from a sixth grader, or motivation from an eighth grader, you are likely to be disappointed. Adjust your plans to fit the age group.

Make it fun. In these days of high-stakes testing, school is serious business, and our students feel the pressure. It's okay to sing a silly song "just for fun," and even a flash-card review of treble-clef notes can be entertaining if you call it a "game." Plan activities that teach through active participation, and show by example that being a musician is enjoyable. Relax and smile, and your students will too.

Consider that two short activities are better than one long one. Attention spans in middle school are notoriously short. Planning a few minilessons with careful transitions will be more effective than giving one long lesson. If the activity is too long, students won't remember what you said anyway.

Take a deep breath and count to ten. Be very, very patient with your middle school kids. After all, they are *kids*. They act childish because they are children; they act immature because they are not yet mature. The only adult behavior you can reasonably expect to see is your own.

Count your blessings. You may be busy. You may be stressed. You may be frustrated. But you'll never be bored! Count your blessings—it's as easy as multiplying the number of seats in your room by the number of classes you teach.

APPENDIX C

Resources

The quest to find materials and resources appropriate for middle school students is unending, and often very frustrating. Many materials, sometimes even those actually labeled for young adolescents, are either too easy or too hard. The list that follows will hopefully provide you with a few things that you can use in your specific situation. Some resources are for direct student use, while others are helpful textbooks or articles for teachers who work with this age group. This is absolutely not an exhaustive list, but rather just a few things I've found helpful over the years. To avoid duplication, resources listed in the "References" section are not included here.

Print Material

Anker, D., C. Ponder, and D. Santman. *Music from the Inside Out*. Van Nuys, CA: Alfred Publishing Company, 2007. Based on the documentary of the same name, this publication contains in-depth lessons that correlate to DVD excerpts from the film, which are included. Lessons include interactive listening and mapping, composing with found sounds, and creating a personal music timeline.

Barrett, J. R., C. W. McCoy, and K. K. Veblen. *Sound Ways of Knowing*. New York: Schirmer Books, 1997. For anyone interested in an interdisciplinary approach to teaching general music, this book is a must read. With both philosophical and practical applications, the authors manage to maintain the integrity of music as a discipline, while making legitimate connections with other areas of study.

Canfield, J., and M. V. Hansen. *Chicken Soup for the Teacher's Soul*. Deerfield Beach, FL: Heath Communications, Inc., 2002. For those days when teacher burnout rears its ugly head, try this book for a reminder of why we got into this career in the first place.

Carnegie, D. *How to Win Friends and Influence People.* New York: Simon and Schuster, 1936. This book was required reading for me during student teaching, and I've used its ideas ever since. If you find yourself struggling to establish a positive relationship with your students, this book may help point the way.

Fergusson, K. *Musical Mysteries.* Carthage, IL: Good Apple, 1985. This is a good source for creative word puzzles about composers, songs, musicals, and performers. It is really helpful for guest-teacher plans, or when you need to keep your students fully engaged in independent work.

Fulghum, R. *It Was on Fire When I Lay Down on It.* New York: Ivy Books, 1989. Besides just being an awful lot of fun, this book includes a wonderful chapter about the composer of "Jingle Bells," which I like to read to my students just before winter vacation. It's a terrific story about enduring success despite repeated failure.

George, L., and D. N. Baker. *Louis Armstrong Education Kit.* Washington DC: National Museum of American History, Smithsonian Institute, 2005. This is a wonderful resource, filled with lots of background information, great photographs, listening lessons, and a compact disc with recorded examples.

Ginott, H. G. *Teacher and Child.* New York: Avon Books, 1972. This is another book of enduring value. Dr. Ginott understood the despair teachers often feel about their struggle to achieve success despite sometimes overwhelming obstacles. This is a handbook of immediately applicable ideas to turn your music room into a really happy place to be.

Hansen, D. "Writing in the Music Classroom." *Teaching Music* 16, no. 4 (January 2009), 28–30. Written by an authority in the field, this article gives a great overview of how to include writing activities in music class.

Lang, L. and M. French, M. *Lang Lang: Playing with Flying Keys.* New York: Delacorte Press. 2008. A wonderful autobiography of the amazing pianist, this book offers an interesting look at the struggles and triumphs of a virtuoso, and it is written at a middle school reading level.

Marsalis, W. *Jazz for Young People Curriculum.* Van Nuys, CA: Alfred Publishing, 2002. Produced by Jazz at Lincoln Center (in conjunction with Scholastic, Inc.), this curriculum includes student books, a teacher's guide, a DVD, recorded lessons on CD, and lesson scripts on CD-ROM. There is so much material that you will likely need to pick and choose what you present to students. Plan to teach along with the recorded lessons to be sure that students are fully engaged.

Marshall, H. D.. "Improvisation Strategies and Resources for General Music." *General Music Today* 17, no. 3 (Spring 2004), 51–54. http://gmt.sagepub

.com/cgi/reprint/17/3/51 (accessed December 29, 2008). For teachers who are inexperienced with teaching improvisation, this article may provide a starting point.

Novelly, M. C. *Theatre Games for Young Performers*. Colorado Springs, CO: Meriwether, 1985. If you and your students enjoy drama activities, you will find lots of activities here. This book includes warm-up ideas, short improvisation games, and longer activities.

Reeves, D. L., and L. Clasen. *Career Ideas for Kids Who Like Music and Dance*. 2nd ed. New York: Ferguson Publishing, 2007. A guide to all sorts of careers in music, this book could help you plan a unit on careers, or serve as independent reading for interested students. Information is presented in a style that is very approachable for young adolescents.

Regelski, T. A. *Teaching General Music in Grades 4–8*. New York: Oxford University Press, 2004. This textbook promotes an "action learning" approach that seeks to develop musicianship skills in middle school that can continue into adulthood. You may find the information about characteristics of adolescents in chapter 2 to be particularly helpful.

Scott, J. K. "Me? Teach Improvisation to Children?" *General Music Today* 20, no. 2 (Winter 2007), 6–13. http://gmt.sagepub.com/cgi/reprint/20/2/6 (accessed December 29, 2008). This is another terrific article about improvisation, with specific lesson ideas for elementary music programs that can be adapted for middle school students.

Websites of Note

www.menc.org

The website of MENC: The National Association for Music Education, this is the place to go for anything you want to know about music education. It includes online bulletin boards on a wide range of topics, a lesson-plan library of ideas submitted by our colleagues, and a general music section. Visit this site for information about how to join the organization and how to access well-respected MENC journals.

www.intunemonthly.com

At this great site for students and teachers alike, you can read about news, participate in contests, and submit questions to a teen musician. Information is also available about student subscriptions to the print magazine.

www.sfskids.org

This is the kids' website of the San Francisco Symphony. There are interactive games and activities that strengthen understanding of the elements of music and music vocabulary. If you have access to a computer lab or an interactive whiteboard with Internet capabilities, this is a great addition to your program.

www.musicalive.com

This website provides information about a monthly student magazine that comes with a teacher's guide and recorded musical examples. Some material is freely available on the site, such as information about music careers.

About the Author

Elizabeth Ann McAnally began her teaching career at the age of eight, when she gave her first piano lesson to the family cat. Many years later, she earned degrees in music education from Nazareth College of Rochester and Columbia University Teachers College. She is delighted to have spent the past eighteen years working with young musicians in Philadelphia, where she is very busy, but never bored! She teaches general music at Woodrow Wilson Middle School, is codirector of the school's 175-voice choir, and serves as lead teacher for her department. She has presented sessions at state, division, and national MENC conferences, where she speaks about urban education and middle school general music. She is a contributing author of *Teaching Music in the Urban Classroom*, and her work also appears in *Teaching Music* and curricula for the Philadelphia Orchestra school concerts.

Made in the USA
Middletown, DE
31 December 2016